Lambelet/Riesterer

Egyptian Museum Cairo

Lehnert & Landrock, Cairo
Kurt & Edouard Lambelet

90 YEARS L & L

Photographs: Lehnert & Landrock, Succ. K. Lambelet, Cairo
Text: Peter P. Riesterer, Zurich. Revised and updated: Roswitha Lambelet
Translation: Dr. Britta Charleston
Legal Deposit Number: 9748/1994
I.S.B.N.: 977 - 243 - 004 - 5
Printed: NUBAR PRINTING HOUSE CAIRO EGYPT

Art Treasures of the Egyptian Museum in Cairo

For nearly a century, since the first organized excavations, Egypt has been the centre, from late autumn until spring, of those countries of ancient oriental culture which not only have a mild, dry climate but also a significant social history. Before the time of Alexander's oriental campaigns the Greeks already knew about this culture. Herodotus (484-425 B.C.), the "Father of History", wrote a lively account of the country on the Nile and we know from other great Greeks that they travelled to the temple sites and "immortalized" themselves on numerous monuments by carving their names on them.

It was, above all, the prodigious stone memorial buildings, the pyramids and the temples, which attracted the people of the occident, and it is still the same today. After the Roman era (30 B.C.-395 A.D.), Egypt disappeared, as it were, entirely from the occidental field of vision. The mud deposited by the annual flooding of the Nile and the desert sand-drifts buried numerous ancient relics and Egypt's once significant position thus sank into oblivion.

Although all the great civilized nations had their share in the later exploration of Egypt, France deserves special mention in this connection: Napoleon's campaign (1798-1801) served as a starting-point for the deciphering of the hieroglyphics by J.F. Champollion (1822). During the course of fortification works at Fort St. Julien in Rosetta on the Delta, an unknown soldier found a black basalt stone, the "Rosetta Stone", one side of which was polished and engraved. It bore various kinds of characters, in three columns: hieroglyphic, demotic and Greek. A translation of the Greek text produced the contents of a dedication by the priesthood of Memphis to Ptolemy V (196 B.C.); the other groups of characters were persuaded to reveal their meaning after considerable effort on the parts of various scholars, but the actual deciphering of the hieroglyphics was first to be achieved by Champollion after much careful study and comparison.

The cultured world continued to show enthusiastic interest in the numerous ancient relics, whose origins date back to many thousands of years ago, and which enable us to draw certain conclusions regarding the times of the Pharaohs. Some of them have been unearthed again from the mud and the desert sand and others have been preserved, only slightly damaged, on the sites upon which they were originally built.

Every year a large crowd is attracted to Egypt and the interest which was once the explorer's prerogative now draws ever-widening circles of people who stand in wonder, often perplexed, at the profusion of the works of art with which they find themselves confronted. It is just as if the ancient Egyptian era had, in our own day, come to life again before our eyes - even if in a different way. Indeed, according to modern research, it has many things in common with our own age. Ancient Egyptian art has drawn closer to us and become more comprehensible for us during the last few decades; the exhibitions of art treasures from the Egyptian Museum, loaned to Europe and America, have been of great assistance in this respect. Scarcely anyone who goes to Egypt does not include one or more visits to the Egyptian Musum in Cairo. This notable collection of art treasures of predynastic and Pharaonic times can be a very profound experience for the beholder.

At first, the objects found during the earliest excavations were housed in a small museum in Bulak. The collection owes its development to the first excavator and archaeologist who went to work systematically in Egypt - the Frenchman, Auguste Mariette-Pascha (1821-1881). In 1850 he was sent to Egypt as an official of the Louvre and there engaged in successful excavating and collecting activities, above all in Memphis (Serapeum) and Abydos. The museum that was founded under his direction, on the instructions of the Khedive, was the forerunner of the famous Museum in Cairo. Mariette was succeeded by Gaston Camille Maspero (1846-1916), also a Frenchman and professor of archaeology at the "Ecole des Hautes Etudes" (1869) and at the "Collège de France" (1874). After 1880, he stayed in the country of the Nile on various occasions as Director of the "Mission Archéologique en Egypte" and as Director-General of the "Service des Antiquités". In 1886, E. Grébaut assumed this post, followed by J. de Morgan in 1892 and V. Loret in 1897; in 1899, Maspero resumed the directorship, which was taken over in 1914 by P. Lacau and in 1936 by E. Drioton; since 1952, the Museum has been directed in an exemplary manner by Egyptian scholars.

Apart from the numerous exhibition rooms which are open to the public and filled with precious objects from various millenia, storehouses and rooms shelter vast quantities of treasures and finds which are reserved exclusively for purposes of research. New acquisitions come in, year by year, from excavations or by purchase. The dry desert sand preserves these treasures and is continually revealing valuable works of art, as did also - until 1971 - the areas that have partly had to be evacuated for the construction of the new dam above Aswan.

The ground-floor contains the most important and massive monuments, dating from the beginning of the Ancient Egyptian era up to late Roman times, treasures which are often incomprehensible to the layman: paintings, statues and reliefs which indicate the worship of gods, the belief in a life after death, and a transcendental world, buildings and ships all dovetailed into an established religious order. It was in the wooden sun barge, or bark, the "Sun Boat", that the god-king journeyed, according to the Ancient Egyptians' conception of the Other World, to the "beautiful West", to the holy abiding place of the dead, where he would be restored to life.

In the "Great Gallery", on the upper floor, with the treasures from the tomb of Tutankhamun, are the coffins of kings and priests, furniture, household effects, vessels, manuscripts and sacred objects artistically wrought in pure gold; there are also two rooms which house the natural science collection and the kings' mummies.

Today there are over 6000 finds exhibited in the Egyptian Museum in Cairo. Of these, 41 masterpieces of Ancient Egyptian art from the periods of the Old Empire, the Middle Empire and the New Empire, which are always explained in detail by the Museum guides, have been selected for reproduction in the first part of this book. The funeral treasures of Tutankhamun are the subject of the second part of this volume.

Between Plate 1 and Plate 41 there lies a period of 3100 years, during which high culture gradually evolved, underwent changes and then died out again. For purposes of comparison, this period is as long as our own western civilization, which had its origins in Greece, embraces both the Roman period, the Middle Ages and the Renaissance, as well as our own times. In order to learn to understand Ancient Egypt, we must go back more than 5000 years as we look at its remains and try to imagine the early period of a civilization and culture that had already passed its apogee when hunters in Europe were still roaming the swamps in search of food during the period following on the Ice Age.

Just how far advanced this civilization and culture actually were in Egypt at that time is shown by the Egyptian calendar, which is divided into three seasons: flooding, sowing, and harvest, each lasting four months. This is based on the observations believed to have been made as early as 4242 B.C., of the star Sirius (Sothis), with its early rising on the Egyptian horizon at dawn and the beginning of the Nile floods connected with it. It is also from the Ancient Egyptians that we have learnt to divide time into periods of 24 hours, with days and nights each lasting 12 hours. They also found out how to make a kind of paper from the pressed stems of the papyrus reed, and an "alphabet (originally) comprising 24 letters". Their writing device was a brush-like instrument or reed. They played music and their dancing was refined; they played a board-game similar to our chess, and lived in well-tended houses set in artistically laid-out gardens, dressed in linen, and produced works of art from precious metals and semi-precious stones.

No other people of antiquity has left, in the form of pictures, the written word, statues and buildings, such a comprehensive and objective picture of itself as have the Egyptians. Their earthly existence runs its course within an established religious order, and both in pictures and in the written word they also give the first indications of the early occidental peoples with whom the Egyptians came into contact.

We have before us a splendid example of the earliest unfolding of the human intellect and its creative ability: "The birth of historically recorded civilization from an as yet unformed pre-historical existence, the beginnings of state discipline and administration, of science and technics, are here immediately palpable", declares Professor H. W. Müller, the well-known Egyptologist. The ascent of mankind and the unfolding of the human intellect are nowhere so clearly perceptible as in the country of the Nile.

The Old Empire (2700-2190 B.C.)

This period was preceded by various civilizations. They left behind them dark-red fired and polished clay vessels decorated with white paintings of subjects from the animal world and, later, bright-red fired clay vessels with red paintings of ships and, at the same time, they left the rock pictures in Wadi Hammamat. The palettes decorated in relief, votive offerings of the kings, date from the year 3000 B.C., and the invention of hieroglyphs and the beginnings of "the ordered reproduction in relief and plastic according to established proportions", can also be dated to this period. Stone vessels and handicrafts achieved a magnificent golden age even before the beginning of the Old Empire. In the Cairo Museum are, among various other precious objects, a make-up palette with a representation of a bull's head, clay vessels, alabaster bowls and King Narmer's victory stelae (1). King Djoser (3rd Dynasty) had the first memorial building, the Step Pyramid, built by his master-builder, Imhotep, in the region of Sakkâra; a little later, the pyramids of King Cheops, King Chephren and King Mycerinus (4th Dynasty) were constructed and the 5th Dynasty heralded the introduction of the Sun Cult as the national religion.

Some of our illustrations show objects from this period, which achieved a zenith of artistic representations carried out in relief. The cross-legged scribe (2) holding a papyrus scroll is a portrait of a higher official very much aware of his dignity and by no means "merely" a literate subordinate. The irises of the eyes of the 50 cm (20") high limestone figure are of inlaid crystal; the green outlines of the eyelids are of copper, and a bronze stud represents the pupil. The limestone figures (3) are about 1.20 m (48") in height and were made a little earlier. Rahotep held high offices under King Snefru as high priest of Heliopolis and also as commander-in-chief of the army; his wife was a member of the court. As her name, Nefert, indicates, she was known as "the beautiful one". She wears a white, close-fitting gown, a brightly coloured necklace, or collar, a wig reaching down to her shoulders and a head-band of floral design. The prince is dressed in a short apron and wears an amulet on a chain about his neck. The short moustache appears to have been the fashion during the 5th Dynasty. In Rahotep and Nefert we have before us a rare and beautiful representation of a couple - in accordance with artistic convention, the male and female figures are differentiated by the application of a darker or lighter colour. The eyes are of inlaid quartz in both the portraits, and there are hieroglyphs painted on the backs of the cube-shaped seats.

In contrast to other ancient peoples, the Egyptian woman occupied a higher and more assured position. She enjoyed rights similar to those of the man and, in the cult of the dead, the woman also had "a right to eternal life". In the pictures, she is depicted by her husband's side and of the same size.

The Pharaohs were equals of the gods - the name "Pharaoh" derives from much more recent times and was hardly used prior to 1000 B.C. Sometimes the king is shown wearing a head-cloth (4), sometimes with the high White Crown of Upper Egypt (5), sometimes with cloth head-dress and uraeus (24), or with the "Blue Crown" (30), or, as "Ruler of Both Lands" with the double crown, consisting of the "Red Crown" of the Delta and the "White Crown" of Upper Egypt. In addition to this, the falcon-headed Horus is assigned to Chephren - a rare representation; the portrait-statue in diorite of the seated monarch (4) is one of the masterpieces of the Egyptian royal statues, which never again reached such heights of expressiveness. On the lion-legged throne, the unity of the two countries is symbolically expressed in the lotus flowers and the papyrus, the water plants of Upper and Lower Egypt.

The green stone representation of King Mycerinus between two goddesses (5), which was found in the "Valley Temple" near Giza, is smaller, about 98 cm (approx. 39") high. The king stands emphatically in the centre of this group of three figures. The figure of the god-king, with his ceremonial beard and royal apron, his left leg slightly forward, stands in sharp contrast to the Goddess Hathor, with the solar disc between the cow's horns, and the Goddess of a Province on the right, both of whom have a slightly peasant-like, even vegetative effect. Manly strength and dignity are expressed by the King's whole bearing. We have a self-assured, but more modest bearing in the figure of Ateti (8). Humbler and more submissive, with his gaze turned towards the spiritual world, a figure of the Priest of the Dead and Ka-Aper, priest and high state official, known as the "village magistrate" or "Sheik-el-Beled" (13), affords the contrast of his corpulence to the youthful figure of (12). He was given the name of "village magistrate" by a labourer engaged in digging, who, upon the discovery of the figure, which is 44 inches high, is alleged to have exclaimed spontaneously, "He looks exactly like our village magistrate!".

Among the figural representations, the working men and women, such as the maid-servant brewing honey beer (11), or the family pictures occupy a position which does not greatly surprise us. The extraordinary thing about the representation of the dwarf Seneb (10) is that, in spite of his deformity, he reached a high position and achieved a title and high offices. The Egyptologist Professor W. Wolf points to the difficulties of combining within a group-sculpture in the round the dwarfish Seneb, his normally-built wife and the two children, difficulties which the sculptor has overcome in a masterly and, at the same time, original manner: "Any of the usual methods of composition was automatically excluded because of the inequality of the body structures. He therefore placed the dwarf cross-legged on a cube-shaped seat, thus making his deformity and lack of stature less noticeable, and placed his wife at his side in the normal position. As this arrangement then resulted in a gap in front of the seat, which again drew attention to the inequality of the couple, he placed here the two children, a boy (left) and a girl (right), who just reached to the height of the seat, thus affording a substitute for the father's legs." Thanks to various representations and, not least, to the excellent reliefs from the *mastabas*, the private graves of higher officials, we know a good deal about life and habits in Ancient Egypt. These reliefs depict masterly scenes of secular life and we not only recognize the musician (middle section, 15), but also the flute and the harp, the instruments then in common use. Besides the harp, the oldest instrument, we recognize the lute, later the lyre and the trumpet. A double oboe and a double clarinet were as well known as the drums, the tambourine, sistrel (rattle) and other instruments. The flute, for instance, consisted of a reed.

Music gladdened the hearts of gods and humans alike thousands of years before our era and dances were performed at banquets and feasts.

The Middle Empire (c. 2040-1785 B.C.)

At the end of the 6th Dynasty, after internal confusion had led to the disintegration of the State and the intellectual world of the Old Empire, King Mentuhetep II, who introduced the Middle Empire, brought about the reunion of the whole of Egypt and the renaissance of Egyptian art. In the valley of Dêr el-Bahri, royal burial-grounds were laid out and the pyramids near Dahschûr, together with a new residence in the vicinity of the Fayûm, were constructed. Sculpture and the goldsmith's art reached their zenith; under the dominion of King Amenemhet III, the art of portraiture achieved excellence. The present state of science and research permits us to draw few definite conclusions about this era. The Egyptologists confirm the statement that the strong tendency towards private ownership of land - "with which a great degree of individual liberty was connected" (Helck/Otto) - was deliberately abolished and the land reverted to the State. "It appears to have been a tradition inherited from the 11th Dynasty that the kings of the 12th Dynasty, unlike those of the Old Empire, no longer conducted their military campaigns with the conscripted provincial militia, but had professional soldiers. "We know from the contents of the graves what these soldiers looked like and what sort of weapons they carried (17), just as we have models which make it easier for us to understand the domestic work (16), the fishing (18) and the water traffic (19) of that time. The Nile fish (18) have not become extinct in the meantime - the fishermen still pull them ashore today. Since time immemorial, these fish have constituted a part of the daily food, particularly that of the poorer sections of the population; at a later period, however, the consumption of fish was temporarily forbidden.

The statuette of the maid-servant in the coloured dress (20) is delightful - she is also described as a bearer of offerings. She carries on her head a box or a basket containing four pots and in her right hand she carries a duck. The steward Amenemhet (22) sits for his portrait on a seat by a table. The master of the house and his wife welcome their guests beside the high pile of gifts.

The Middle Empire is also described as a period of the finest intellectual perfection (Brunner-Traut), of significant literature and subtle art. Although the museums of Boston, Paris, London, Berlin, Copenhagen, Vienna, Leyden and New York have in their possession important sculptures from this era, we nevertheless have two very significant representations in the Cairo Museum which corroborate the above statements - the cedar-wood statue of King Senusret (Sesostris) I (21), who wears the "White Crown" and also the one side of a pillar from a chapel of King Senusret in Karnak, on which the king is embraced by the god Ptah, the "artist" or "sculptor". The written characters are clearly legible. Twice above the King's head and, again, at the god's side, we recognize the oval frame which surrounds the King's name - the cartouche. Senusret was known as the "Man of the Strong", a name which was borne by three kings of the 12th Dynasty.

The New Empire (1552-1069 B.C.)

Once again the unity of the country disintegrated and the Hyksos, a foreign Asiatic people, assumed dominion in Lower and Middle Egypt, the duration of which exceeded 100 years, until the princely dynasties residing in Thebes threw off the foreign yoke.

The New Empire is often described as the "Era of World Power". Egypt extended right up to the River Euphrates and all the way to Nubia. A lively building activity began once more to develop and not only temples, rock tombs and obelisks date from this time, but, more important, also royal and private graves richly decorated with wall-paintings. Queen Hatshepsut built a terrace-temple at Dêr el-Bahri, which gave new impulse and a new direction to art in general; it is often described as "ageless" and still astonishes us today with its clear, severe lines.

Egyptology names three artistic directions which existed during the time of this Empire: it describes the first phase of the development of art (until the reigns of Hatshepsut and Tuthmosis III) as the "Severe Style", the second phase under Amenhotep II and Tuthmosis IV as the "Mature Style" and the third phase, which began in western Thebes under Amenhotep III and became more and more refined, is called the "Soft Style". The short era of Akhnaton in El-Amarna is spoken of as a period of "overripe" artistic forms.

The Rameses, who later administered the country, distinguished themselves by their numerous buildings between Abu Simbel and the Eastern Delta ("Rameses Town"), while the Ptolemaic era followed after the incorporation of Egypt into the world empire of Alexander the Great. As the burial-grounds were already plundered during the reigns of the kings, the only indication we have of the pomp and splendour of the funeral rites of those far-off times are the almost intact grave-goods from the tomb of Tutankhamun. Compared with other royal tombs, Tutankhamun's is described as "modest" in view of his brief reign. What immense treasures must have accompanied the other Pharaohs on their last journey - unless, of course, Tutankhamun was a special case?

There is a magnificent treasure-chest (23) in the Museum, the jewel-case of Amenhotep III, which, apart from the cartouches and the written characters, also bears the hieroglyph representing " Eternal life". On the other hand, we may well ask ourselves where the sculptor obtained the material for the white marble statuette (24). Did seafaring Cretans bring it from Greece? In this portrait-statuette, which is only 14" high, we see King Tuthmosis III in sacrificial pose, and also sacrificing to the god Amon (25), who wears the double-feather crown. This picture gives us an idea of a funeral chapel such as often found in Thebes. They are artistically decorated with secular scenes.

The "Queen of Punt" (28) is a section of the "Punt Journey" of Hatshepsut's fleet in Dêr el-Bahri. We do not know with certainty where the homeland of these foreigners lies. They climb up ladders to their "honeycob" dwellings, but there must have been an abundance of gold and incense in their country, which is presumed to have been south of Somaliland. "The Queen with Steatopygia" (second from the left) is followed by servants bearing gifts. The inscriptions of the temple wall say that the ship is loaded with apes, incense trees, ivory, gold, timber, leopard skins, baboons and dwarfs. Queen Hatshepsut had the incense trees planted in front of her terrace-temple. She transformed her gardens "into Punt" and "the palace was flooded with the perfume of the god. All its perfumes were from Punt".

The Ancient Egyptians ascribed a special significance to the funeral cult and the belief in the "afterlife". According to their religious philosophy, the soul of the deceased not only returned to the spiritual world, it could also return to the body and stay there. The body was, therefore, embalmed. Offerings were made to the dead, who, from the "beautiful West", could re-enter the world of the living by a false door (8) in the East.

Later, the dead were laid in richly ornamented coffins (38) and *usheptis* (36), tiny figures, were laid beside them in order that, should the deceased be called upon to work in the "other world", they might answer and perform his work for him. These "answerers" - later also known as "the Master's Servants" - are a part of the conception of the next world that existed at that time. The work or duties which they had to perform in the next world is indicated by the inscription which they bear.

From the time of the 18th Dynasty onwards, written collections of proverbs were laid with the deceased in the grave; these were described as the "Book of the Dead" (39 and 40) . It is only in the "Books of the Dead", of the New Empire that pictorial representations are to be found: "In the presence of Osiris on his throne and the forty-two judges, the heart of the deceased was weighed against the symbol of the maat (an ostrich feather). Thot officiated as scribe; Anubis operated the scales, a crocodile-headed monster threatened to devour him who was not recognized" (Helck/Otto).

We know that, at the end of the 5th Dynasty, the dead king was identified with Osiris. From that time date the first indications that Osiris was called the "God of the Dead" and "Lord of the Judgement Court". Anubis, the god in the shape of a dog, also known as the "Jackal-headed One", whom we recognize in the lower illustration (40), under the scales on the left, is not only a "cemetery and funeral god", he also officiated at the Judgement Court as one of the great gods of the "other world", together with Thot, the "Master of Knowledge and Calculation", who, as a god, became the "patron saint" of the sacred writings. In Antiquity he was known as Hermes trismegistos, a great teacher of Egyptian civilization, "who showed people that the entire physical world was as divine writings and taught them to appreciate the physical world". The goddess of the Sky, Nut, is also to be seen in the same representation (40). She touches the earth with her finger tips and bends her star-studded body in a wide arc over her husband, the god of the earth, Geb, who is lying on the ground. She also gives birth to the sun and the stars. In the cult of the dead, the rôle of a motherly protectress falls to the "goddess of the thousand souls" - the stars are regarded as being her soul.

Akhnaton (30) turns towards the sun. He does not only honour the sun, but he had it proclaimed that: "There is only one god and he is called Aton, the sun, who sustains us and all things." Sculpture took on new forms under Akhnaton; the king and his family are represented under the sun's rays terminating in outstretched hands (33). The limestone bust of the beautiful Nefertiti, the wife of Akhnaton, gives unique expression to Ancient Egyptian art and culture. This portrait-bust from the sculptor's workshop in Achetaton (today in the State Museum of Berlin-Dahlem) has attained world renown by reason of its beauty. Less known is her likeness in brown quartzite (32), upon which traces of the chisel are still recognizable. A fascinating masterpiece, ageless and of a high artistic order.

The rendering of birds and other animals in papyrus thickets also belong to the Amarna period (29). They are decorative and naturalistic. These finds are in many ways just as important as are those of the Old Empire. It is not possible to draw comparisons; each era has its own particular duty and mission.

We stand in admiration and awe before the works of art whose creation lies thousands of years in the past. They emanate the spirit of that time "in which all the conditions of what we call thought were fulfilled in their entirety" (Spiegel).

	Main events	Main Kings	Dyn.	Time - table	
3000					3000
	Unification of Egypt	Narmer	1	**Archaic**	
	Begin of hieroglyphs and calendar Foundation of Memphis	(= Menes?)			
			2		
2700		Khasekhem			2700
	Step pyramid at Sakkara	Djoser	3	**Old**	
	Sphinx △∧∧ + at Guiseh	Cheops Chephren Mykerinos	4	**Kingdom**	
	Sun temple at Abusir △ at Sakkara; 1st Pyr. texts	Userkaf Unas	5		
			6		
	Ruled 94 Years; desintegration of the monarchy	Pepi II			
2200					2200
	Coffin texts Flourishing of literature			1st Intermediate Period	
2040					2040
	Tomb at Thebes △ at Dahshur △ at Hawara Drainage of the Fayum	Mentuhotep Senusert III Amenemhet III	11 12	**Middle** **Kingdom**	
1785			13 17	2nd Intermediate Period	1785
	Introduction of horses and chariots	Hyksos Kings Sekenenre			
1552					1552
	Expedition to the Land of Punt Empire: Euphrates-4th cataract Cult of the unique god Aton Tomb found unspoilt in 1922 by H. Carter	Hatshepsut Tuthmosis Akhenaten Tutankhamun	18	**New** **Kingdom**	
	Temple at Abydos Battle of Kadesh	Sethi I Ramses II	19		
	Temple at Medinet Habu	Ramses III	20		
1069	Unspoilt tomb at Tanis	Psusennes	21		1069
	Seizure of Jerusalem	Sheshonq	22 23	**Late** **Period**	
		Piankhi	24-25		
	Serapeum in Sakkara Circumnavigation of Africa	Psammetic Nekao	26		
	Completion of a canal from the Nile to the Red Sea	Cambyse Darius	27		
		Nectanebo	28-30		
332					332
	Foundation of Alexandria with the Pharos (= light house) Temple of Edfu and Philae	Alexander Ptolemy Cleopatra		**Ptolemaic** **Period**	
30					30
0	Temples at Esna + Philae Persecution of Christians Foundation of monasteries	Claudius Diocletian		**Roman** **Period**	0
395					395
	452: last text found in Demotic at Philae			**Byzantine** **Period**	
641					641
	Amr Ibn el Ass conquers Egypt			Arab Conquest	

The Funeral Treasure of Tutankhamun in the Egyptian Museum in Cairo

As Akhenaten had only daughters, he married one of them to the little prince, Tut-ankh-Aten, whom he had elected to be his successor. As the government gave up the exclusive cult of the Sun-god Aten and reverted to the old gods after Akhenaten's death, the young king (Pharaoh). changed his name to Tut-ankhamen ("the living image of Amen or Amon"). It was in his name, now usually written Tutankhamun, that the decree re-instating Amon in his former splendour and rights was promulgated. Tutankhamun, the last descendant of the XVIIIth dynasty, died after a reign of only nine years, not yet twenty years of age. His successors showed no gratitude for his willingness to revoke the Amarnan heresy, for they obliterated his names and that of Akhenaten from the list of the kings. Interesting as is the story of this delicate boy-king, who grew up an adherent of the heresy and, for reasons of state, later apostatised from it, be would certainly never have had any great prospect of becoming the most famous of all the Pharaohs. Yet his tomb, which was provisionally built in the Valley of the Tombs of the Kings, was spared the fate of the other Pharaohs' tombs, since it fell into oblivion together with his person. Not until the year 1922 did Howard Carter (1873 - 1939), who was excavating in the Valley of the Kings with the material support of Lord Carnarvon (1866 - 1923), discover the completely buried tomb. Everything was still in it: the coffins, one inside the other, the statues of the king, the golden treasure, the funerary equipment, the trappings, the golden treasure, the funerary equipment, the trappings, the gilded shrines, objects made of alabaster and faience - an incomparable body of material for the study of Egyptian art and the cult of the dead.

Jean Yoyotte

Tutankhamun

The story of this king, who lived in Egypt about 1350 B.C., occupied the throne for some nine years and died young, can only be conjectured. The birth and life of Tutankhamun are shrouded in mystery, and there are more than enough hypotheses. First, there is the almost intact tomb to the west of Thebes, discovered in the Valley of the Kings by Howard Carter on November 4, 1922, which still today baffles scholars, and which raises the question: If burial treasures of such immense value were piled up in this small sepulchre of an unimportant Pharaoh, what riches must have been contained in the tombs of the great Pharaohs before they were plundered? Then there is the early death of the King, which some scholars think was "caused by violence"; there is also the strange injury on the left cheek - a rounded depression in front of the lobe of the ear, covered with scurfy, colourless skin. The questions concerning his birth and origin still remain unanswered, and indications pertaining to the events and the people at the end of the XVIIIth dynasty are lacking.

This should not surprise us, since we know that Tutankhamun's predecessor, Akhnaton or Akhenaten (Amenophis IV, in Egyptian: Imn-htp = "Amon is content") deposed the old gods together with the influential priesthood; he left the temple site of Thebes (the present-day temple complex of Karnak, near Luxor), which was consecrated to the god Amon, in the sixth year of his reign, and founded a new capital, Akhetaten (Amarna), in Middle Egypt, substituting for the old conception of the gods a belief in Aten, the visible Solar Disk, or Globe.

The Amarna episode ended in chaos. Egypt, which had become a world power under Tuthmosis III, some fifty years before the time of Amenophis IV, suddenly found herself on the threshold of a new spiritual epoch with its "heretic" king, Akhenaten. "Akhenaten was not only born before his time spiritually, but he tried to bring about a premature spiritual birth at the risk of his life, attempting something that could not have been realised in the course of one man's life, but only in the course of time itself. He was himself broken in the process", says Ernst Uehli.

Tutankhamun was born into this Amarnan epoch.

Who was Tutankhamun?

We know that Tutankhamun's reign came at the end of an epoch that saw the rise of a new religion, which was wiped out again soon afterwards. It signified a break with the old traditions, with the earlier art and culture, and with Egypt's policy of expansionism. Those who had been deprived of their former privileges became the inexorable enemies of the new religion and the new régime. The empire gradually disintegrated. The army and the deposed clergy began to grumble. Both were waiting for the great moment, of which we unfortunately know very little. Moreover, what we do know is as shadowy as Tutankhamun's life itself.

"... the first problem to be solved is that of chronology", writes Christiane Desroches-Noblecourt in her vast work *Tut-ench-amun: the life and death of a pharaoh*: "More than fifteen authors who have studied the period place the reign of Tutenkh*amon* (his birthname modified after his return to Thebes) at slightly different dates, although they all agree that it lasted nine years. For some, those years are from 1369 to 1360 B.C.; for others, from 1357 to 1350 or 1349. A third school of Egyptologists hold the view (which we believe to be closest to the truth) that Tutenkh*aten* came to the throne in 1352 or 1351 and died about 1344 or 1343. He was succeeded for some four years by the 'Divine Father' Ay, whereupon General Horemheb seized the throne. This, however, is pure surmise, since there is still no single piece of documentary evidence to establish where Tutenkh*aten* was born, or at whose court he grew up."

Among the objects found in Tutankhamun's tomb, a certain number point to a relationship with Amenophis IV - Akhenaten and his mother, Queen Tiye (or Tyi). There would seem to be a certain portrait likeness between the King and these two. A small gold statuette was also found in the tomb representing Amenophis III, the father of Akhenaten, crouching in the attitude of the solar child "as if to show his oneness with the son in whose flesh he was to be reborn, in order to perpetuate himself, according to the order of things". But a lock of Queen Tiye's hair was also found, "touchingly enclosed like a mummy in its own little sarcophagus" ... " beside the effigy of her husband". "Other objects in the tomb also allude to the King's parents, such as the alabaster pitcher bearing the pharaonic names of the Malkata couple" (Amenophis III and Tiye).

Are a statuette of Amenophis III and Tiye's lock of hair eloquent proof of their parenthood of the young king?

"Without wishing to be rash, it does therefore seem probable that before the end of the year 35 of Amenophis III, the Great Royal Spouse Tiye gave birth to her last child, Tutenkh*aten*, in the harem at Malkata. Egyptian custom decreed that the child's birth name should be chosen by his mother from words she had uttered when she was delivered - in the case of a prince destined for the throne this name was used until his coronation. Later a second name was added to his style. When he uttered his first cry and the 'breath of life' entered into him, Tutenkh *aten* was stamped with the mark of the Atenist heresy, and his youngest sister, born a year or two earlier, had also been dedicated to the Globe, ruler of Akhetaten, the capital where they were both soon to be taken to live with their young nieces.

Since everything in that strange period is a problem, it is not surprising to hear that learned circles still disagree about the meaning of the young prince's name. For all Egyptian names were short sentences, intended to place the newly born under the protection of a god. Only the seven fairies of Hathor, who welcomed the infant into the world, could tell us what Tiye really meant by the words which, more than 3000 years later, became generally known. Some say 'powerful is the life of Aten' or 'gracious of life is Aten'; yet others 'living image of Aten'. And an entirely new theory offers the translation: 'All life is in Aten's hands'. Thus philological opinion remains divided upon the name which the Egyptians ceased to use from the day of the young King's coronation as *Nebkheprure*" (Desroches-Noblecourt).

The Ancient Egyptians' Funeral Belief

As far back as our knowledge reaches, the belief in a life after death has been alive in the Egyptians. In spite of certain more luminous forms of the dead person, and also the conception of the Ka (an idea that is characteristic of Egyptian thought, though the interpretation of it is still disputed) who, as the bearer of all life, is also the bearer of a future life - the dead man lives on in his human shape. The preservation of the physical uninjuredness and the supply of food necessary to the maintenance of the vital processes are therefore indispensable prerequisites for the belief in the beyond. The cult of the dead and the grave-gifts are intended to secure this life after death.

Bonnet

This definition of the belief in the after-life enables us to understand the lavishness with which the tombs were provided with every kind of cult object.

The idea of an eternal and actual death was incomprehensible to the ancient Egyptian. After crossing the threshold of death, he lived on in the "beautiful West" and presumably the purely material conception of giving him his entire property in the grave so that he might enjoy eternal life was a further development from this idea. The dead man was not buried merely with drinking-vessels and dishes for food - these being indispensable objects found also in the graves of the poor. His earthly riches surrounded him in the kingdom of the dead; he could even sign a contract with the Ka-priests while he was still alive, stipulating that they should provide him regularly with food-offerings at the grave or in the temples of the dead. The belief in an after-life that was similar to life in this world naturally required that the body itself should be preserved - the dead person was mummified. The corpse was washed and anointed with oil; the cavities left in the body after the inner organs had been removed were filled with resin or resinous substances, and the extracted viscera were preserved in Canopic jars (72). At the end of the mummification process, the corpse was wrapped in long strips of linen. Tutankhamun's mummy was enclosed in three coffins (45-48) and four shrines (page 24). The head and shoulders of the young monarch were covered with a gold funerary mask (42, 43), actually a portrait-effigy of the King.

The sarcophagus was accurately orientated on an east-west axis, and there were 143 burial objects entombed with it. In his original notebook, Carter records that the head was encircled by a gold diadem set with precious stones, with the cult symbols of the Northern and the Southern Kingdoms. A gold band ran across the breast to the ears to hold the King's head-dress in place. Round the neck there were two kinds of symbolical collars and twenty amulets grouped in six layers and between each of these layers were numerous linen bandages. The breast was ornamented with 35 objects disposed in 17 groups, and consisting of four golden collars with Nekhabet vultures and Buto serpents, then more metal collars, eight in all, each separated from the next by linen bands. In an eleventh and twelfth layer, further pieces of jewellery, such as pendants and pectoral ornaments in the form of vultures and scarabs (85), and heartshaped pendants of gold with the symbols of Osiris and Isis. In the linen cloth over the thorax and the abdomen were two groups of golden finger-rings. Both forearms with a mass of golden bracelets and bangles right down to the wrist. Each finger encased in a gold sheath. Gold rings on the second and third fingers of the left hand. Above the body, ten objects distributed in ten layers separated from each other by linen bandages, among which a gold amulet, eight gold circlets in four pairs, a gold waist-band or girdle encircling the waist, obliquely across the abdomen a richly ornamented dagger of gold housed in ornate ornamental gold sheath. On both girdles cylinder-like attachments for ceremonial pendent tails. Under the mummy, ritualistic animals' tails of faience beads. A ceremonial apron made up of seven gold plates, extending from the abdomen down to the knees. Underneath, a finely-wrought dagger with an iron blade in a gold scabbard. Attached to the diadem and forming part of it, on the right the Nekhabet vulture, left, the Buto serpent, seven more circlets in three layers of wrappings above the upper part of the thighs. The feet in wrought-gold sandals, each toe in a separate gold sheath.

The sevenfold encasing in four shrines and three coffins in a yellow quartzite sarcophagus that surrounded Tutankhamun's mummy, the sumptuous extravagance of the inventory and cult objects and the immense wealth of gold give a further mysterious picture of this Pharaoh. To the question whether the more powerful kings were buried with still greater pomp, there is yet another, which is also posed by Ernst Uehli in "Kultur und Kunst Ägyptens" *(Culture and Art of Ancient Egypt):* Is Tutankhamun not a special case as regards burial and magic?

There are some scholars who answer this latter question in the affirmative, and who believe they can interpret it as a case of cult-magic: Akhenaten and his works became the victim of a magic curse. The name of the sunking was obliterated and became anathema. Tutankhamun, on the other hand, became the "victim" of a magical glorification of his mummy; he became the tutelary god for those whom he left behind in the world of the living, for the priests of the god Amon, once again powerful, and for their religious community and their cult. The gold mummy was to strengthen and enhance their mummy-magic.

At first sight this appears rather strange. Tutankhamun as tutelary genius? This theory becomes comprehensible if we study the belief in the gods, the conception of the Beyond, and the magic practised by the ancient Egyptians, that is to say, their whole religious conception. The grip that magic had on the ancient Egyptian - as Hans Bonnet, the expert on the science of religion, states in his *Reallexikon der Ägyptischen Religionsgeschichte* (Encyclopaedic Dictionary of the History of the Ancient Egyptian Religion) - is a distinctive characteristic of the spiritual structure of the people of those days. His whole thought and his faith bore the impress of magic. His everyday life was entirely steeped in it. Man could master magic and make use of it for his own ends, for instance, to promote Tutankhamun to be the tutelary genius of the priests who had returned to power, but who still felt insecure. We must not forget that in Ancient Egypt religious worship was still largely magical, and it was entirely by means of magic that the burial paraphernalia and the numerous texts from the "Book of the Dead" gave the dead man the power to maintain his life in the next world.

Age-old forces that still lay dormant in the ancient Egyptians have been lost. Much, therefore, that once existed seems strange and unreal to us, and we can penetrate it only by profound, scholarly study.

Plan of the tomb

On November 4, 1922, Howard Carter stood at the entrance to the tomb; on November 25, the first sealed doorway was demolished, and on November 29, the second sealed doorway was ceremoniously opened.

Tomb-robbers, who had twice entered Tutankhamun's last resting-place, had penetrated to the Antechamber (South Chamber), which was piled high with 171 objects and pieces of furniture. Some of these objects had been thrown about and left in disorder. The thieves had also entered the Side-Chamber (Annexe), and a scene of confusion met Carter when he first looked in. The Burial Chamber was opened on February 17, 1923. It had also been penetrated by the plunderers; the Treasury contained the most precious pieces, which had served for the funeral rites; there, too, some of the boxes had been rifled.

The tomb is situated on the west bank of the Nile near Luxor in the Valley of the Kings (Biban el-Muluk).

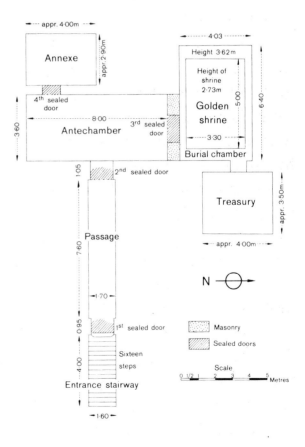

Original disposition within the tomb chamber of Tutankhamun

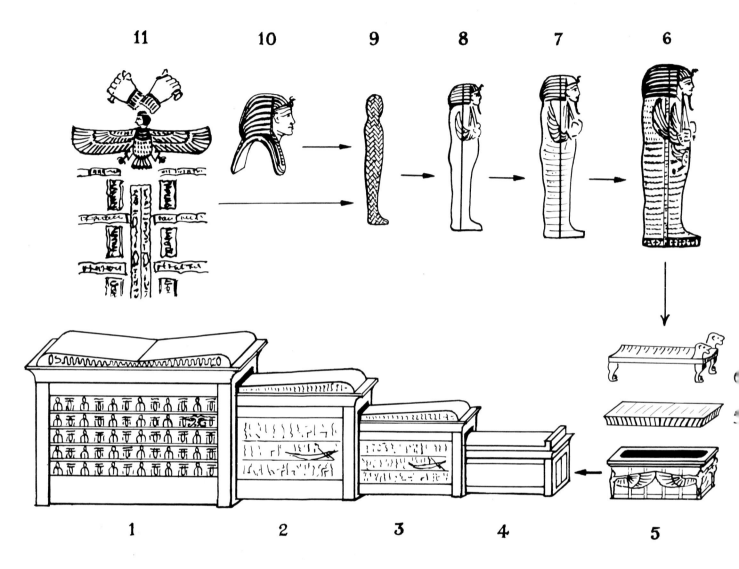

1-4: *Shrines of the sarcophagus Nr. 1322-1319 Gallery 7,8*
 5: *Quartzite sarcophagus*
5 a: *Granite lid Thebes, tomb nr. 62*
 6: *External coffin Thebes, tomb nr. 62*
6 a: *Bier Nr. 1118 , Room*
7-8: *Second and internal coffin Nr. 222, 219 Room 3*
 9: *Mummy, in Thebes*
10: *Golden mask Nr. 220 Room 3*
11: *Jewelry found on the mummy Nr. 336, 224, 266 Room 3*

Tutankhamun's Tomb: Discovery and Treasure

Howard Carter, the discoverer of the tomb, had excavated in the "Valley of the Kings" for several winters in succession, being constantly intrigued by the stratification of the debris at the foot of the tomb of Rameses VI, which suggested the presence of a tomb. He may have thought of Tutankhamun.

On October 28, 1922 - no excavating was done during the summer heat - Carter again arrived in Luxor. On November I, he engaged workmen and immediately began to search at the north-east corner of the tomb of Rameses VI, trenching southwards. Already on November 4 his workmen stood at the beginning of a cutting which was situated about three feet below the entrance to the tomb of Rameses VI and about the same depth as the present-day valley-floor. The cutting appeared to be a step, the first of a whole flight leading downwards. On November 5, Carter was convinced that he had discovered the upper part of a sunken stairway. One by one the steps came to light, and soon a doorway, plastered over with mortar and bearing the traces of seals, became visible. The seals were those of the Royal Necropolis: The Jackal and the Nine Prisoners. On November 26, Carter had reached a second sealed door, the seals of which were those of Tutankhamun and the Royal Necropolis.

He writes:

"Great was our feeling of awe when we made the discovery, cleared the stairway and steep descending passage, and entered the Antechamber, when we beheld in that hypogeum for the first time the splendour of the Imperial Age in Egypt, fourteen centuries before Christ. The gorgeousness of the sight, its sumptuous splendour, made it appear more like the confused magnificence of those counterfeit splendours which are heaped together in the property-room of some modern theatres, than any possible reality surviving from antiquity. The effect was bewildering, almost overwhelming. Moreover, the extent of the discovery had taken us by surprise. It is true that we had expected to find the tomb of Tut-ankh-Amun in the Theban Valley, for reasons already pointed out in the first volume, but our supreme surprise was to find it, for all intents and purposes, intact.

Unlike the other royal tombs in the Valley which had all been completely plundered, only a few fragments of their furniture being left, this tomb was for practical purposes intact, save for the early depredations of a few metal robbers. To this fact our great surprise and good fortune were due. Had the tombs of the great Pharaohs of the Theban Empire been found in a similar condition, the tomb of Tut-ankh-Amun would have seemed of comparative insignificance, except that the art of his period would still have remained an outstanding feature.

We soon realized, however, that our first duty was to record, clear and preserve the contents of the Antechamber before attempting any other task. The objects in this chamber were in such dangerous contact that their removal, without causing damage, must be, we saw, a task of some difficulty. It took the greater part of the first season to transport them to the laboratory, where the work of recording, preservation and packing was eventually carried out. It was only after this chamber had been cleared that we were able to penetrate and solve the mystery of the inner sealed door.

Though a shrewd guess anticipated what might be beyond that mysterious sealed door - guarded by two imposing sentinel figures of the king (53), black and gold, armed with mace and staff - little did we expect the impressive sight revealed as, stone by stone, the masonry blocking the doorway was removed. First, to all appearance, a wall of gold met our gaze, affording no clue to its meaning, until, as the aperture became larger, we realized that what was barring our view was an immense gold shrine (44), and that we were now at the entrance of the actual burial chamber of the King. - An almost incongruous miscellany of objects and furniture, caskets and beds, chairs, footstools, chariots and statues, filled the Antechamber. These were heterogeneous enough, yet exhibiting in not a few instances, a kindly art full of domestic affection, such as made us wonder whether, in seeking a tomb of a Pharaoh, we had not found the tomb of a boy. From strange ceremonial couches fashioned in the form of uncanny beasts (61, 63) - demon deities comparable to Greek satyrs - Thoueris (62), 'The Great One', the favourite of the people, in shape partly hippopotamus, partly crocodile and partly feline, personifying 'Protection'; Hathor, 'The Abode of Horus', in the form of a cow (64), the goddess of pleasure and love, the mortal and immortal nurse; and

'The Terrible Goddess of War', or it may be of 'The Chase', fashioned like a lion or, perhaps, to be more accurate, a cheetah - from these we passed into the severely simple Burial Chamber occupied almost entirely by its great sepulchral blue and gold shrine.

It would be difficult to describe our emotions when for the first time the light of our powerful electric lamps flooded the Burial Chamber - 'That silent seat of a Lord of the West' - illuminating as it did the walls on which were painted representations of Amen-tît, the catafalque drawn on a sled by the chief nobles of the land, King Ay before the Osiride Tut-ankh-Amun, and lighting up the immense shrine overlaid with gold, and inlaid with brilliant blue faience tiles, nearly filling up the entire area of the chamber - a space of only one or two feet separating it from the walls on all four sides, while its great roof reached almost to the ceiling.

When we found the first step, when we opened and obtained our first glance at the crowded wonders in the Antechamber; when this sealed door leading to the Burial Chamber was broken through, and when we saw, for the first time in the history of archaeology, one of the great sepulchral shrines under which the Pharaohs of Egypt were laid - these, unless my memory misleads me, were the thrilling moments of the first part of the discovery".

Although Carter's work of excavation was beset with difficulties on all sides, he was able to complete his task. In retrospect he admits:

"...and, glancing back now at the second season's work, it seems that our interests were never more deeply stirred than when concentrated on the contents of that simple sepulchre. The task, however arduous, then became enthralling. Our first duty was the removal of the various objects around the shrine, to be followed by the dismantling of the latter with its nest of shrines, shielding in their centre the great yellow quartzite sarcophagus.

Around the emblems, symbols, furniture and monuments associated with Egyptian sepulture, especially when seen for the first time, there always hovers the spirit of mystery and awe, and it was when the lid of the noble sarcophagus was gradually raised, revealing the magnificent outer coffin of the King within, that one of these supremely moving moments was again ours. But life is full of painful disappointments, and it was here that our labours of that winter were destined to be brought to an untimely end." But the other work, too, making an inventory of the burial objects and, at all, the examination of the mummy, was not without difficulties: "Now with archaeological work the reverse to that which is anticipated almost always occurs. The opening of those elaborate coffins, without causing them harm, proved an intricate undertaking. The procedure which we were obliged to adopt in the examination of the King's mummy was, to say the least, disheartening.

Judging from the external appearance of Tut-ankh-Amun's outer coffin, from the preservation of the royal mummies formerly discovered, and now in the Cairo Museum, after all the depredations they had suffered, one was led to expect that this untouched king would be in almost perfect condition. Unfortunately, that was not the case. We found him in a terrible state. There was every proof that care had been taken in his mummification; he was swathed in masses of the finest cambric-like wrappings; he was literally smothered with every kind of ornament and amulet; he was enclosed in a solid gold coffin; but, the very custom of those last burial rites proved his destruction. The mummy as well as the gold coffin had been subjected to consecration unguents that had been poured over them in great quantity. Those unguents were of the nature of fatty matter, resin, and possibly wood-pitch, originally in a liquid or semi-liquid condition. In the course of time the decomposition of those unguents acted destructively upon the contents. The consolidated residue of the unguents also formed a hard black pitch-like mass, which firmly stuck both the mummy and its mask to the bottom of the coffin; and no amount of legitimate force could move them. The mummy had to be examined as it lay *in situ* in the coffin. Thus any systematic unwrapping for which we had hoped, was rendered impossible. The charred linen bandages, which fell to powder at the touch, had to be removed bit by bit. Moreover, the conditions rendered the use of X-rays impossible. Nevertheless, though the undertaking was not such a clean piece of work as one would have wished, I am glad to say little, if any, data was lost, and all the objects were eventually preserved. The preservation of the latter, the ornaments and amulets, meant many months of work. It necessitated the experience not only of a chemist but of a jeweller. But for the anointing unguents, Tut-ankh-Amun, his wrappings and accessoires, in that gold coffin, would have been practically as perfect as when first placed there.

Another of our difficulties was to extricate the gold coffin (45, 47) from the shell of the second coffin (46, 48). The unguents poured over them had completely filled and consolidated the space between the two coffins, thus sticking them fast together. This problem was eventually solved, and we now have the two perfect and most wonderful coffins yet found.

It is of archaeological importance to note that all three coffins were not only Osiride in form, but their decoration was of the feathered type. The king's mummy we found neatly made and fashioned to symbolize Osiris. Covering the head and shoulders was a magnificent mask of beaten gold (42, 43). The outer wrappings were embellished with heavy gold trappings which had somewhat suffered from the action of the unguents. Enclosed within the wrappings were 143 objects, comprising a diadem, daggers, girdles, personal jewellery and amulets. Three of these objects introduced an astonishing feature. They were of iron, which I believe is the first authentic purposed introduction of that metal into Egyptian civilization. It coincides approximately with the period when iron began to overtake bronze in Syria. Another most important historical fact was revealed by the king's mummy - his age of death, and his remarkable structural resemblance to his father-in-law, Akh-en-Aten, which throws light on his probable parentage. It is also of interest to note that there was neither a true heart-scarab upon the body, nor as yet have we found any trace of documents in the way of papyri, either of religious or of literary king. The material discovered in this last season has been transported to the Cairo Museum, where most of it is already on exhibition. The king's mummy, re-wrapped, will remain in his tomb enclosed in his sarcophagus".

Tutankhamun's burial treasure is displayed in the Egyptian Museum in Cairo. Every year, thousands of visitors stand in admiration before the magnificent jewellery and the splendid show-pieces. The little that is reproduced in this book gives an idea of the immense wealth and profusion of the treasures. All this is the expression of a religious cult that is in close connection with the ancient Egyptians' conception of life beyond the grave.

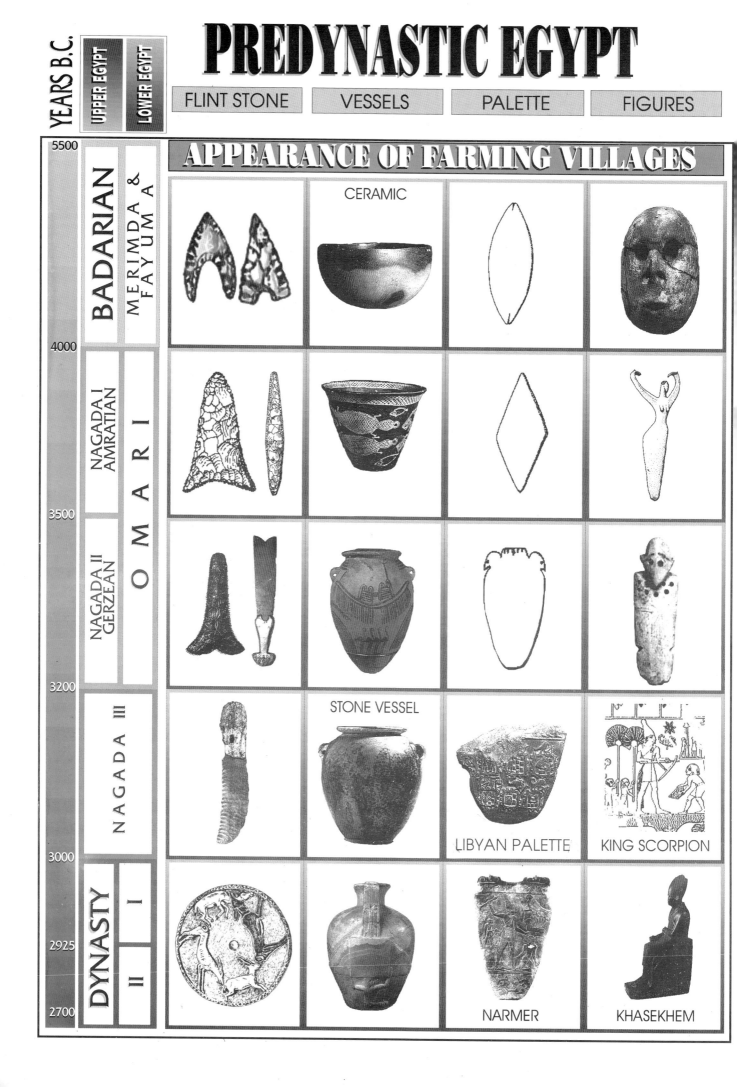

PREDYNASTIC EGYPT

YEARS B.C.

UPPER EGYPT · LOWER EGYPT

FLINT STONE · VESSELS · PALETTE · FIGURES

APPEARANCE OF FARMING VILLAGES

CERAMIC

STONE VESSEL

LIBYAN PALETTE · KING SCORPION

NARMER · KHASEKHEM

BADARIAN — MERIMDA & FAYUM A

NAGADA I AMRATIAN — O M A R I

NAGADA II GERZEAN

NAGADA III

DYNASTY I · II

5500 · 4000 · 3500 · 3200 · 3000 · 2925 · 2700

Old Empire 2700 - 2190B.C.

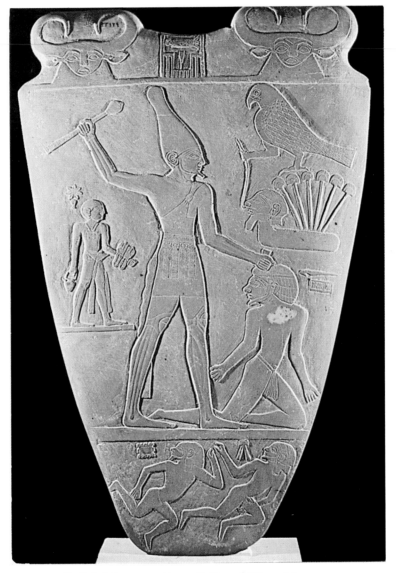

I Schist cosmetic palette of King Narmer

1. DYNASTY, HIERACONPOLIS

2. Limestone statue of a scribe with papyrus scroll - 4./5. DYNASTY, SAKKÂRA

3. Prince Rahotep with his wife, Princess Nefert - 4. DYNASTY, MEDÛM

4 King Chephren, builder of the Second Pyramid at Giza - 4. DYNASTY, GISEH

5 King Mycerinus between Goddess Hathor and the Goddess of a province

4. DYNASTY, GISEH

6 Frieze of geese painting on plaster, from the tomb of Itet - 4. DYNASTY, MEDÛM

7 Painted relief showing fishermen jousting - 6. DYNASTY, SAKKÂRA

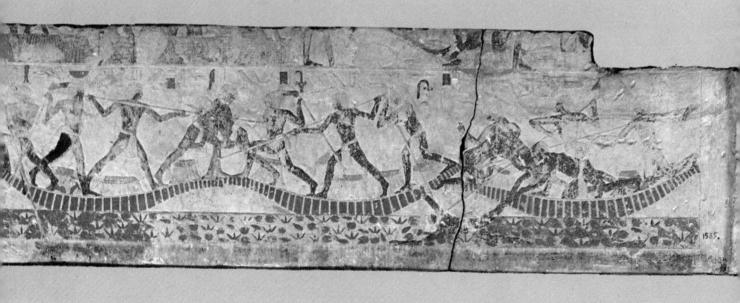

8   Painted false door (limestone) from the tomb of Ateti - 6. DYNASTY. SAKKÂRA

9   Head of King Userkaf; Aswan granite - 5. DYNASTY, SAKKÂRA

10   Dwarf Seneb with his family - 5. 6. DYNASTY, GISEH

11   Woman brewing beer: painted limestone statuette - 5. DYNASTY, SAKKÂRA

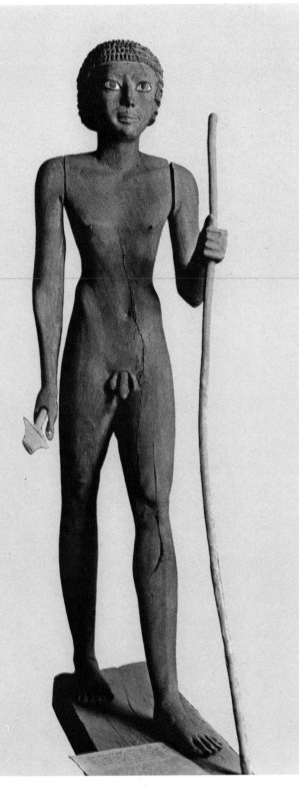

12   Wooden statue of a young man

6. DYNASTY (?). SAKKÂRA

13   Sycamore-wood statue of the "Sheik-el-Beled"

5. DYNASTY, SAKKÂRA

14   Gold head of a mummified hawk

5. DYNASTY, HIERAKONPOLIS

15 Scenes of a feast; tomb of Net-heft-Ka - 5. DYNASTY, SAKKÂRA

16 Spinners and weavers at work; from the tomb of Meketre - 11. DYNASTY, DÊR EL-BAHRI

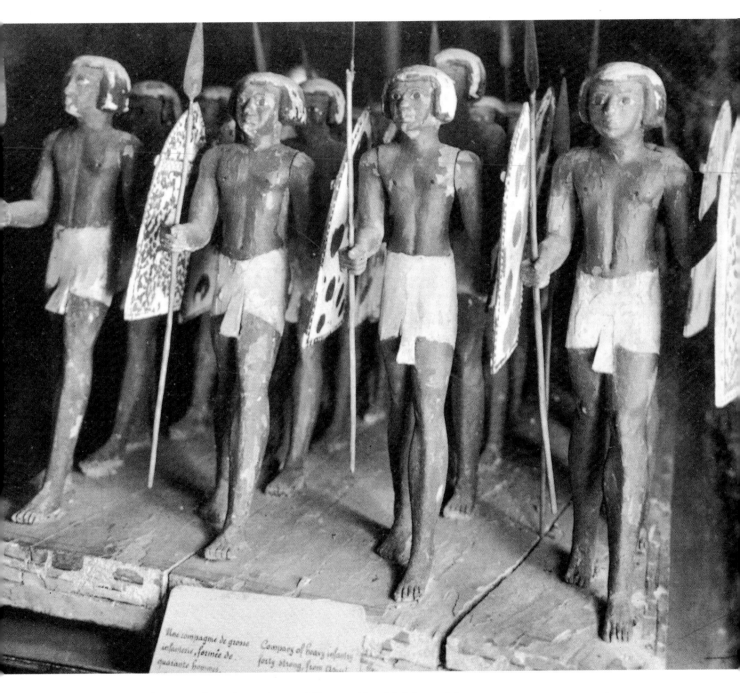

Une compagnie de grosse
infanterie, formée de
quarante hommes.

Company of heavy infantry
forty strong, from Ass...

17 Group of 40 Egyptian soldiers with shields and lances - 12. DYNASTY, ASSIÛT

18   Fishing-boats dragging a net with Nile fish: from the tomb of Meketre

11. DYNASTY. DÊR EL-BAHRI

19 Model boat with linen sail; from the tomb of Meketre - 11. DYNASTY. DÊR EL-BAHRI

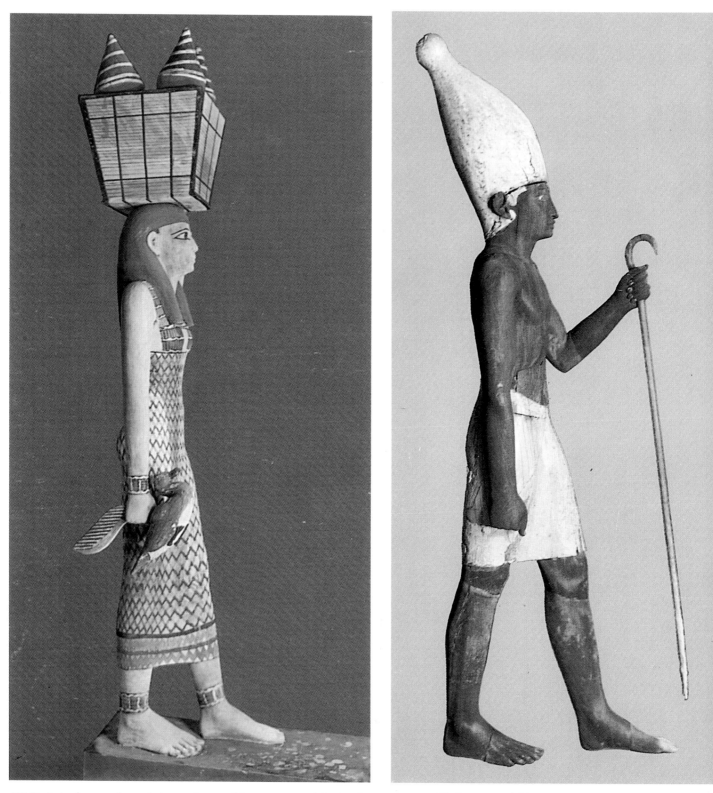

20 Painted wooden statue of a maid-servant with duck

11. DYNASTY, DÊR EL-BAHRI

21 Statue of King Senusert (Sesostris) I

12. DYNASTY. LISCHT

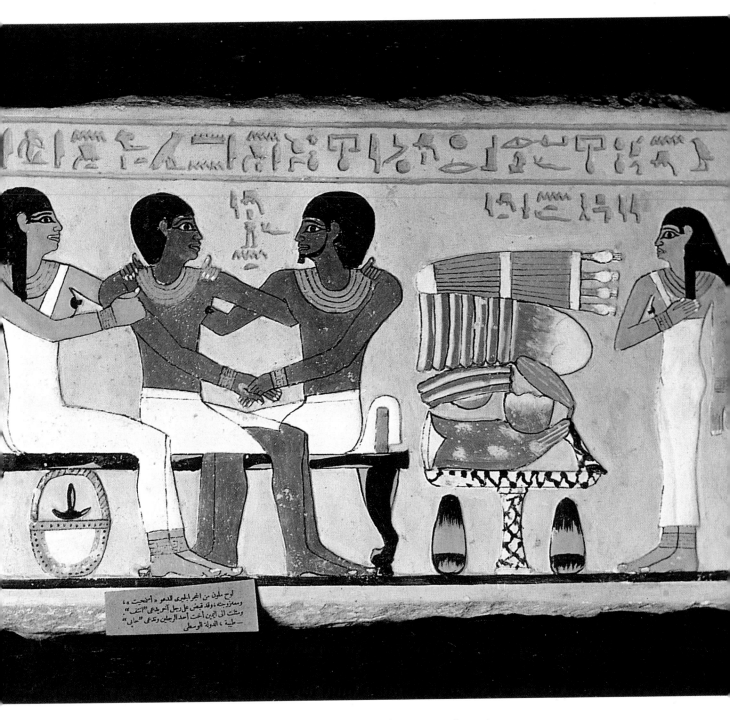

22 Part of painted limestone stela of steward Amenemhet - 11. DYNASTY. ABYDOS

23 Jewel-chest of King Amenhotep III - 18. DYNASTY, BIBAN EL-MOLUK

24 White marble statuette of King Tuthmosis III - 18. DYNASTY, DER EL-MEDINE

25 Painted sandstone chapel of King Tuthmosis III - 18. DYNASTY, DÊR EL-BAHRI

26 King Amenhotep II beneath the Hathor Cow - 18. DYNASTY, DÊR EL-BAHRI

27 Black granite stela with victory-poem of King TUTHMOSIS III
18th DYNASTY. KARNAK

28 Queen of Punt, from the terrace-temple of Queen Hatshepsut - 18. DYNASTY, DÊR EL-BAHRI

29 Sedges (Cyperus alopecuroides) and papyrus (Cyperus papyrus) with wild ducks

18. DYNASTY, EL-AMARNA

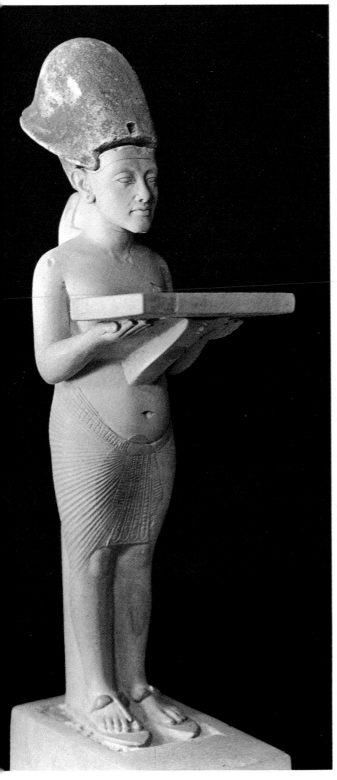

30   King Akhnaton with sacrificial
     tablet and blue crown
     18. DYNASTY, EL-AMARNA

31   Limestone colossus of King Akhnaton
     18. DYNASTY, EL-AMARNA

32   Unfinished quartzite head of Queen Nefertiti - 18. DYNASTY. EL-AMARNA

33   Akhnaton offering sacrifices beneath the solar disk; painted limestone

18. DYNASTY. El-AMARNA

Mummy of King Seti I. 19. DYNASTY, THEBES

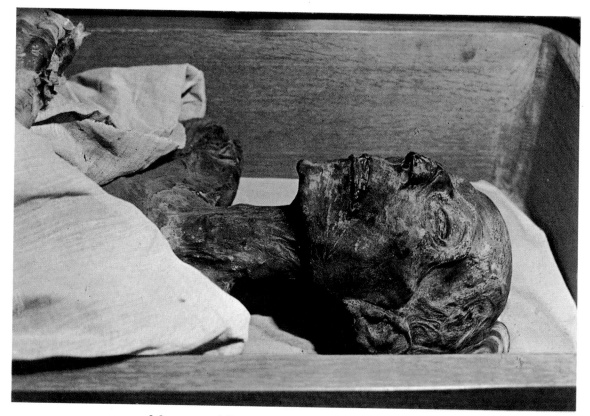

Mummy of King Ramses II. - 19. DYNASTY, THEBES

36 Funeral Statues of the lieutenant Hat and of the noble Ptahmose - 18. dynasty, Tuna / Abydos

37 Procession of priests and dignitaries - 20. DYNASTY. EL-ASASÎF

38 Coffin-cover of Queen Maâtkere - 21. DYNASTY Biban el Molûk

39 Funeral papyrus with texts from the Book of the Dead - 21. DYNASTY, THEBEN

40 Funeral papyrus; Goddess Nut of the Sky with star-studded body

41 Painted gold death-mask. Ptolemaic period, Meir

The Funeral Treasure of Tutankhamun in the Egyptian Museum in Cairo

Plan of the royal tomb

42 Gold funerary mask of Tutankhamun

43   Side-view of King's funerary mask

44   Innermost shrine, heavily gilded

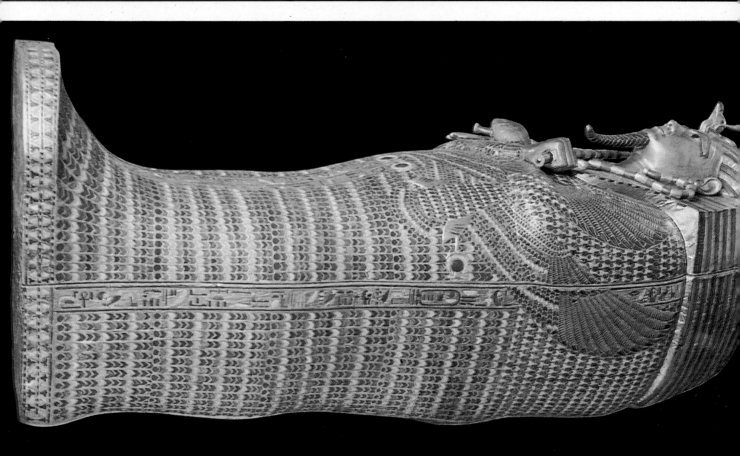

45 + 46 The gold coffin (top) contained the mummy of the King. It was enclosed in the second coffin (bottom)

47 + 48 Left: detail of the richly decorated gold coffin, right: the second coffin

49 Large gold canopic chest

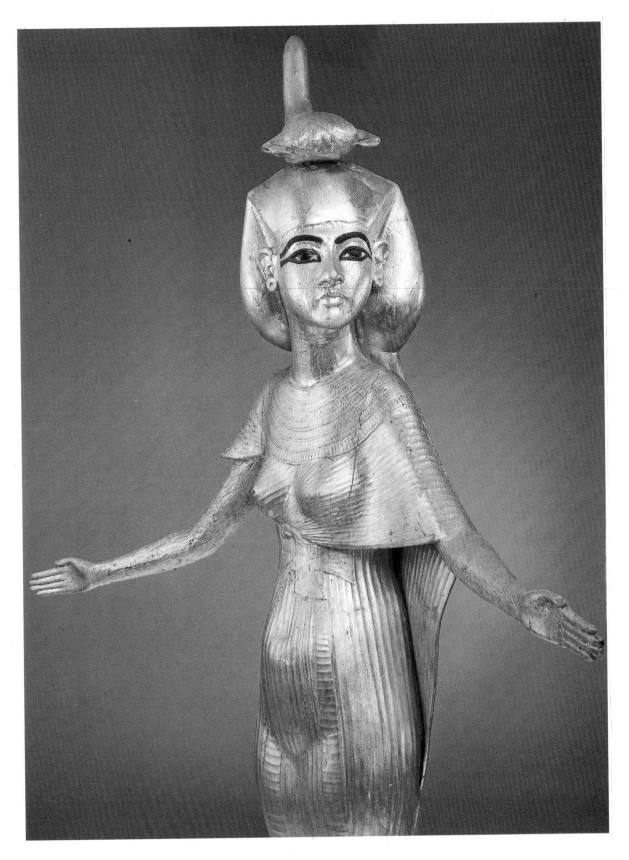

50   The golden statue of goddess Selket

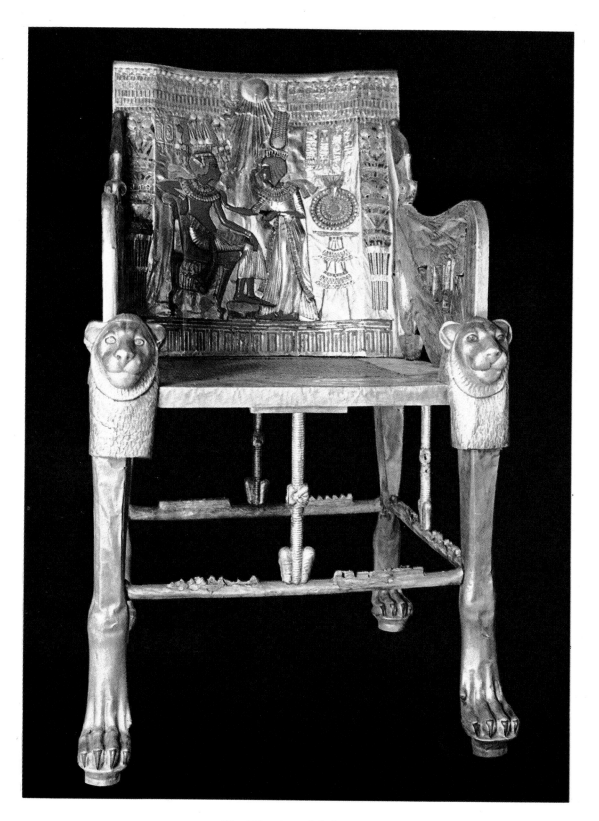

51 King's gold throne

52   Back of throne showing Tutankhamun and his consort

53   Life-size gilded wooden statue of Tutankhamun

54   Anubis shrine with djed and tjet symbols

55 Magnificent painted wooden chest

56   King and Queen on lid of ivory chest

57   Tutankhamun's ecclesiastical throne

58 Richly decorated chair of Lebanon cedarwood

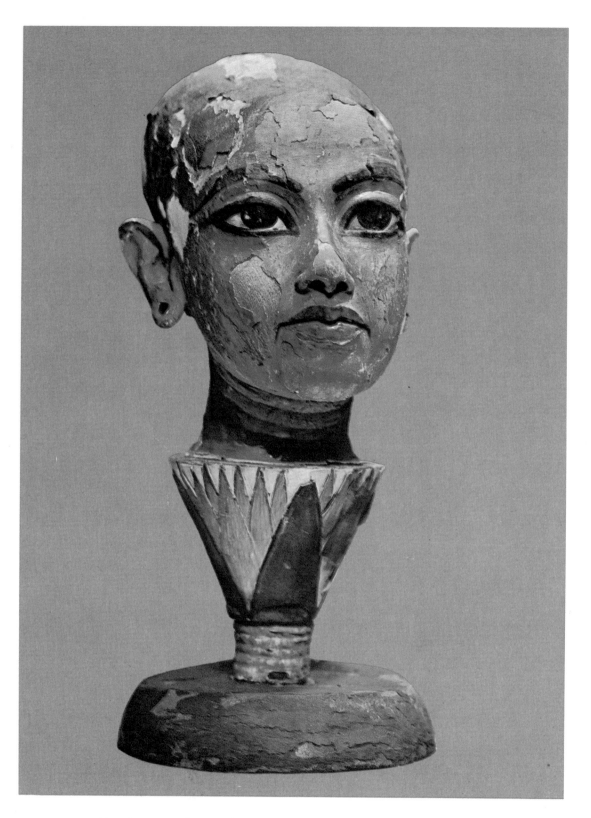

59 Apparently royal portrait, emerging from a lotus-flower

60   Gold statuettes of the King, with the crowns
of Lower (left) and of Upper (right) Egypt

61 Funerary bed in the form of cheetahs

62 Head of a funeral couch; the goddess Thoueris
in the form of a hippopotamus

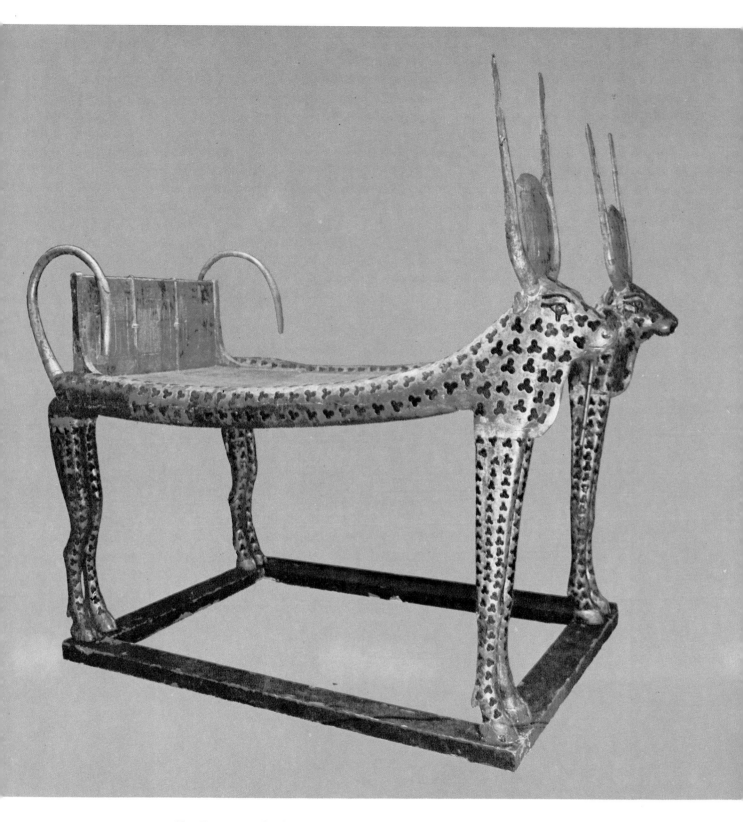

63   Funerary bed in the form of the cow Hathor, with the solar disk

64   Hathor, sacred cow, funerary bedhead

65 Gilded cedarwood ushebtis

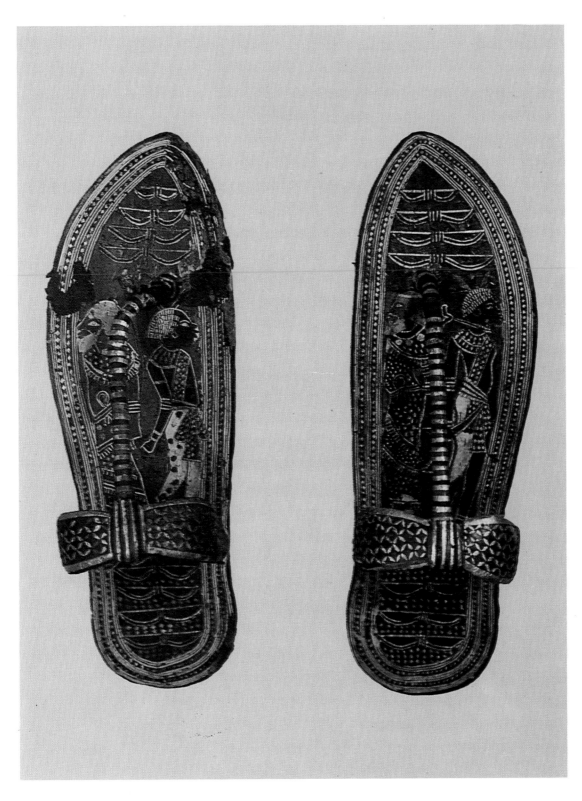

66 The King's state-sandals

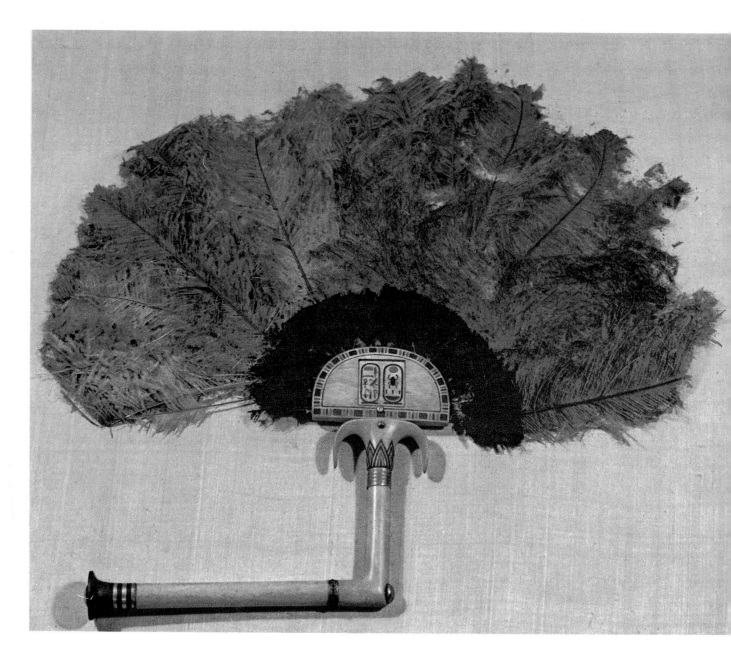

67 Ivory fan trimmed with ostrich-feathers

68   Model of the Pharaoh's bark

69 Folding ivory head-rest

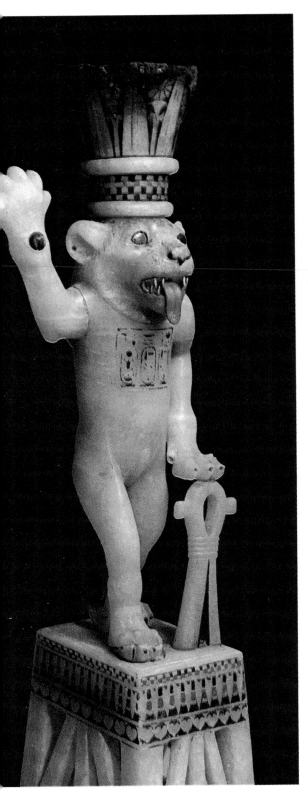

70 The god Bes, with crown
and royal cartouches

71 Unguent jar of the royal couple,
with flower garlands

72 Alabaster canopic chest on gilded sledge

73 Alabaster busts of the King, from the canopic chest

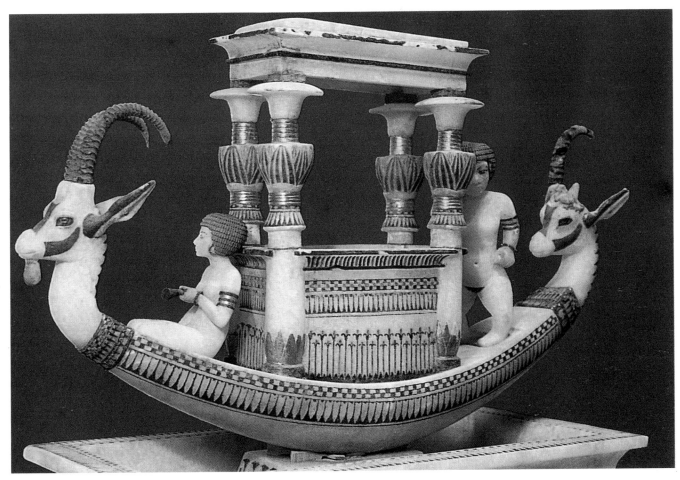

74 Decorative boat of alabaster with canopy

75 Alabaster lamp in the form of lotus flowers

76   Unguent jar in the form of a crouching ibex

77   Alabaster vase with inlaid decoration

78   Alabaster unguent jar decorated with animal scenes

79, 80 Two pairs of earrings from the King's jewel-chest

81   Gold pendant with scarab and baboons

82   Pectoral plate; King between god Ptah and goddess Sekhmet

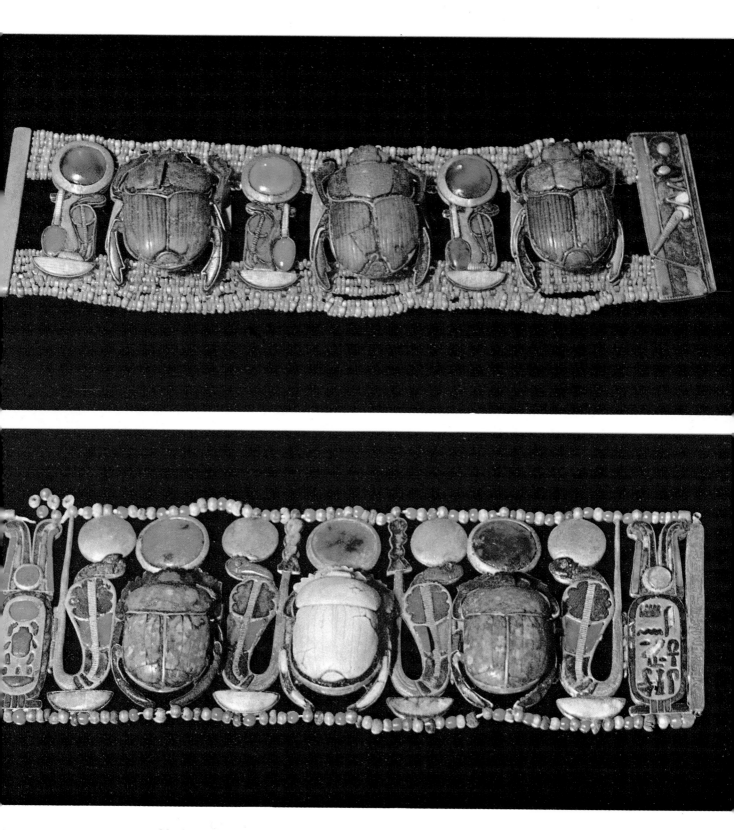

83, 84 Two gold bracelets inlaid with semi-precious stones

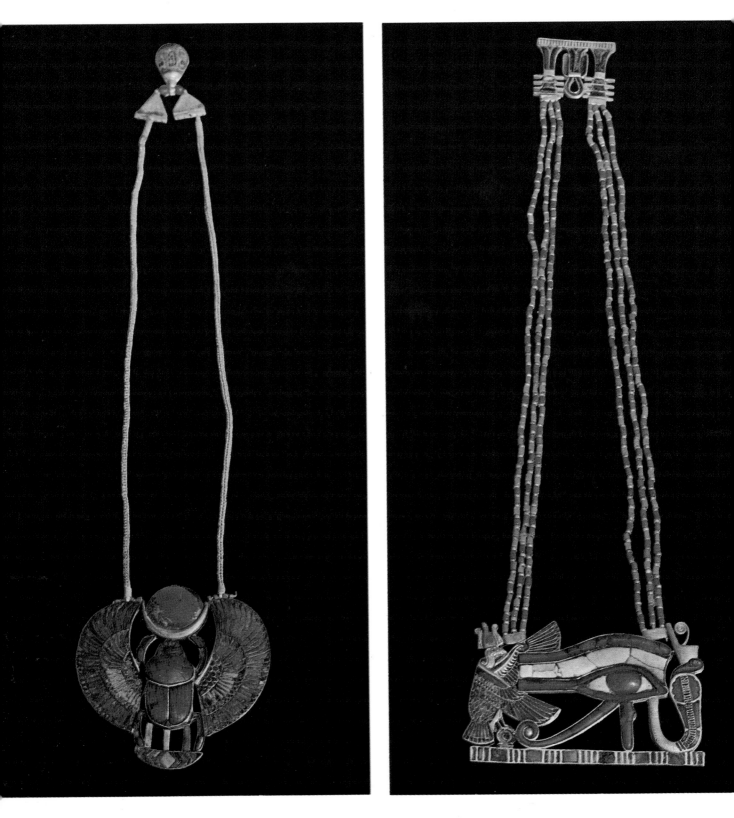

85   Gold pendant in the form of
     a lapis-lazuli scarab

86   Gold pendant with the Magical Eye

Commentaries on the illustrations

1 Schist cosmetic palette of king Narmer, possibly identical with king Menes. The king with the white crown of Upper Egypt raises his mace against a prisoner from the   The falcon, mythological ancestor of the kings, brings in prisoners of the swampy regions, symbolic representation of the conquest of Lower Egypt. Above, between the two Hathor-cow heads, the hieroglyphic name of the king in a rectangle representing the royal palace.

2 A scribe in Egypt was an administrative official, a man in public life, raised above all ordinary people. His was "the noblest of all occupations". To be a scribe was an honour. This scribe with his papyrus scroll was a high dignitary (limestone, about 20 in. high)

3 The statues of Prince Rahotep and his consort Nefert date from the beginning of the 4th dynasty and come from the mastaba at Medûm. The princess is wearing a headband and collar, a linen gown and a wig; the prince has a simple necklace with an amulet. Behind the figures are hieroglyphs - symbols developed from a purely pictorial script.
Rahotep (with moustache) was probably a son of king Snefru. He held the highest offices and, in accordance with ancient Egyptian custom, wears only a short apron (limestone, 48 in. high).

4 The seated portrait-statue of Chephren, the builder of the Second Pyramid, is 66 inches high and is made of diorite. Behind the King's head is the hawk-headed god Horus. As the sky-god and sky-hawk he was equated with the King (to his people the ruler was a manifestation of Horus). On the throne is the emblem of the united realms of Upper and Lower Egypt - papyrus and lotus flower.

5 King Mycerinos, the builder of the Third Pyramid of Giza, between the goddess Hathor and a regional (nome) goddess, above whose head the nome emblem of Diapolis Mikra can be seen. Green slate, about 39 in. high. The King is wearing the crown of Upper Egypt. The goddess Hathor is identified by the sun disk between the cow's horns.

6 One of the most naturalistic examples of ancient Egyptian painting: the frieze of the geese, from Medûm, dating from the early part of the 4th dynasty. The geese on the stucco were part of a painted tomb. The brilliant colours have remained fresh to this day.

7 Jousting with poles from fishing boats was an aspect of physical training - a sport in which the participants, armed with long poles, tried to dislodge and topple each other into the water.

8 The picture shows the false door of a sacrificial chamber (the stele, originally free-standing, is recessed into the wall). It served the performances of rites in tombs and mortuary temples. Its notional purpose was the provision of a link between the living and the dead. The sacrifices and prayers - which were seen as obligations vis-à-vis the deceased - were performed before it.

9 The head of King Userkaf, a pink Aswan granite, is 26 inches high. It was found in the king's mortuary temple near Sakkâra. It was in this period, when the sun cult (the cult of Re) of Heliopolis had become the state religion, that sculpture reached its finest flowering.

10 Pathologically deformed dwarfish Egyptians were predominantly household servants and were able to rise to high rank, as shown in this picture. The limestone group is 13 inches high. Seneb was "the king's friend" and "overseer of the palace"; he was also employed as a priest in the mortuary temples. The true pygmies came to Egypt from the interior of Africa and were so-called "dancers of the god" of the king's "jesters".

11 Besides water, beer was the "national beverage" of the Egyptians, both living and dead; it was also "a drink prized by the gods". Emmer and barley were pounded, moistened, and the lumps lightly baked. This "bread" was softened by soaking in water and, after fermentation, filtered into a pot.

12 From the tomb of Merire ha-ishtef: from the latter part of the 6th dynasty three superbly worked and variously sized works of art survive, known as the "wooden statuettes of a nude young man".

13 The 43 inches tall wooden figure of Ka-Aper, better known as the "village magistrate", represents a priest and a high state official. The quartz eyes are set in copper eyelids. The figure has been known as the "village magistrate" ever since it was found by the excavation workers because it resembled the then local village magistrate.

14 Horus was the principal god of Hierakonpolis. He is represented as a hawk. In this picture he is wearing the plumed crown, two erect ostrich feathers of gold, and in front the uraeus, the serpent symbol of royal power.

15 A painting on limestone showing (at the top) the partly visible legs of Net-heft-Ka, seated at a table laid with fruit and various foods. Below are musicians. In the bottom row are barebreasted dancing girls. The women in the long garments are clapping the rhythm with their hands.

16-19 From the 6th dynasty onwards, wooden statuettes of servants began to appear in the cult chambers. They were placed by the dead man's coffin. The monarch (the 'nome' governor) was accompanied by soldiers with shields and lances (17). There were spinners and weavers (16), men fishing with drag-nets (18) and model boats (19) - all of them realistic models, reflecting a delight in factual, accurate representation. Meketre - from whose tomb the objects in Plates 16, 18, 19 come - was chancellor to one of the last kings of the 11th dynasty.

20 This wooden statue from the tomb of Maktire at Dêr el-Bahri represents a woman in a colourful fish-scale patterned garment carrying offerings. On her head is a basket with four pots, in her right hand a duck.

21 Senusret (Sesostris) I was one of the three kings of this name in the 12th dynasty. The name means "Man of the Strong" (= of the powerful goddess). His pyramid stood near Lisht. Senusret led campaigns against Nubia and engaged in intensive building activity, especially at Karnak and Heliopolis.

22 Representation of a banqueting scene. The table is laid with all kinds of meats and vegetables.

23 Jewel-chests were made of wood with inlays of blue lapis-lazuli, coloured glazes and carnelian. The wood was gilded; sometimes wafer-thin gold-plate was used. In addition to hieroglyphics and cartouches the illustration shows the *ankh* symbol, the life-loop, adorning the lower frieze.

24 Several kings of the 18th dynasty bore the name Tuthmosis (= born of Thot, the god of knowledge and calculation). The statuette of the king is of white marble; its height is about 14 inches. The kneeling king is offering a gift to the deity.

25-26 Sandstone chapel with cow goddess Hathor. King Amenophis II (Amen.
hotep), painted in black (colour of death) is under the head of Hathor in
the prayer position; he is shown again painted in red (colour of life)
drinking from the cow's udder, indicating that he has been adopted as
her son. The chapel contains painted reliefs showing Tuthmosis III and
his wife worshipping Hathor and Amun-Ra.

27 Granite stela with a poem celebrating the victories of Tuthmosis III and
counting the conquered countries. The rhymed words can be seen at the
beginning of each line.

28 One of Egypt's most interesting and fascinating figures, though still surrounded by many historical and personal enigmas, was Hatshepsut. As
Regent she commanded exploratory expeditions to be made to the mysterious Land of Punt. Punt was Egypt's supplier of incense, gold and
pygmies, and must have been situated somewhere on the African shore
of the Red Sea or even further south. The "Queen of Punt" is represented as a fat woman, on the right. On the left are two Servants with gold
ingots .

29-32 Under Amenhotep IV (subsequently Akhnaton) a new art trend
developed, known as the Amarna style from the king's residence at Tell
el-Amarna. This style ran counter to all previous Egyptian attitudes.
Only fragments survive of the painted floors of the palace (29).
Akhnaton had all aspects of his body's shape depicted "realistically"
(31). These greatly exaggerated curvacious shapes are seen also in the
"Little King with offering plate" (30), representing Akhnaton or
Smenkhkare (limestone). One of the most significant finds is the head of
Queen Nefertiti (brown quartzite, 13 in. high) which still shows the
marks of the pointed chisel. The author of this book places this
fascinating timeless masterpiece of sculpture (32) above the painted
limestone bust of Nefertiti in the Dahlem Museum (Berlin).

33   The visible sun disk-Aton-under Akhnaton replaced the Theban deities Amon and Mut, and took the place of imagined gods. The sun disk, with its rays terminating in probing and sometimes giving hands, stood at the centre of hymnic and pictorial representations. Akhnaton's "Hymn to the sun" is a great piece of inspired literature, a hymn to the sun's spirits, unique and outstanding in the millenial history of ancient Egypt.

34   Mummy of King Seti; profaned by tomb robbers (his head was torn off), the mummy still emanes an impression of royal dignity.

35   Mummy of King Ramses II. This pharaoh reigned 67 years and reached the age of almost 88 years. His face carries asiatic features. Hands and feet are dyed with Henna. The skin was coloured in yellow during the mummification; in prevous times a dark-brown colour was used.

36   These grave statuettes, known as usheptis or "answerers", were put in the deceased's tomb so that, whenever he was called upon to perform some work in the hereafter, they could "answer" for him and do his work. Hundreds of them have been found in various tombs.

37   The dignitaries can be identified by their implements and their wigs. Priests are always represented bald or with shaven heads.

38   Biban el Moluk (west bank near Thebes) is associated with the most fantastic grave-robber stories of the 19th century. The inhabitants of this village, situated on the former necropolis of this village, situated on the former necropolis, in 1875 carried out illegal searches of the tombs and sold their finds at random. In 1881 the Government was apprised of this activity. The remaining finds, including those from an "improvised collective grave" were transferred to Cairo, where they can now be admired in the Museum.

39-40 "Book of the dead" is the name given to the collections of proverbs written on papyrus and placed in a dead person's tomb from the 18th dynasty onward. The individual manuscripts vary in lengh and composition. Mythological pictures alternate with realistic ones; above agriculture, below the deceased in front of the jackal-headed judge of the head (left) on a scale, on the right the figures of deities under the starstudded body of Nut, the sky goddess.

41 This death-mask is attributed to the Ptolemaic period and was found on a mummy in Room 14 of the Ptolemaic finds. The reign of the Ptolemies began after the death of Alexander the Great with his general Ptolemy and continued for about 300 years, until 30 B.C., as the "Macedonian dynasty"

42 The gold funerary mask is a portrait of the King and covered the face of the mummy. The *nemset* head-dress with the royal insignia, the uraeus-serpent, or royal cobra, and the vulture, is made of gold inlaid with lapis-lazuli coloured vitreous paste. The eyes are inlaid. The collar over the breast has inlays of lapislazuli, felspar, and quartz . Height 21 in., width 15 1/2 in.

43 Profile view. The funerary mask shows the King probably at about the age when he died. He is wearing the "ceremonial beard", which, according to Bonnet, has no religious or ritual significance. The lobes of the ears are pierced, for the King wore earrings some 4 in. in length (Plates 79,80).

44 Four shrines took up most of the space in the burial chamber. The outermost is 205 in. long, 132 in. wide and 108 in. high. All four shrines comprise some eighty parts and are gilded. The picture shows the innermost shrine, containing the young King's sarcophagus.

45 The third and innermost of Tutankhamun's three coffins (the gold coffin) contained the royal mummy; it is made of solid gold. It is 74 in. long, 20 in. wide and 20 in. high; it was enclosed in two larger coffins. The King is shown as Osiris, holding sceptre and *flagellum* (flail, scourge).

46 The second (mummiform) wooden sarcophagus is covered with gold and decorated with semi-precious stones and coloured glaze inlays (imitations of turquoise). Side view. Length 80 in., width 27 in., height 31 in.

47 Detail of the richly decorated gold coffin (45) embellished with semi-precious stones and coloured glaze.

48 The second coffin seen from above. The central descending band contains the royal cartouches and hieroglyphs (hieroglyphs are pictographic symbols derived from a purely pictorial script).

49 The large gold canopic chest (49) enclosed the smaller alabaster chest (72) which contained four carved alabaster stoppers for the miniature coffins with the King's viscera. Two of these stoppers are shown in Plate 73. Along each of the four walls of the canopic chest stands a goddess: Nephthys guards the lungs, Neith the stomach, Isis the liver and Selqet the intestines. The heart had to remain in the deceased's body.
Height of the canopic chest with sled and canopy 79 in., width 49 in., depth 60 in.

50 The scorpion-goddess Selket protects the viscera (especially the intestines), preserved in the canopic jars, together with the goddesses Isis, Nephtys and Neith. Sublime grace radiates from the harmonious proportions of their bodies, from their expressive and noble faces and from their fine and elegant dresses.

51 Tutankhamun's golden secular throne. The arms of the throne are in the form of two crowned uraeus-serpents whose wings are spread in a protective gesture over the King's names, Above the two front feet of the throne, a magnificent pair of lion's heads. Height 45 in., width 21 in., depth 25 in.

52 The back of the throne depicts the King and the Queen in a room in a palace. The Queen is holding an unguent jar. The sun's rays end in hands which hold out to the royal couple the keys of life, or *ankh*-symbols. Their robes are of silver, the background of gold-plate. Figures: red vitreous paste, blue glaze, inlaid alabaster. Back c. 21 x 21 in.

53 Life-size wooden statue of Tutankhamun, covered with black lacquer and partly gilded. Two such statues stood guard one on either side of the entrance of the burial chamber. Height 68 in.

54 Lid of a wooden chest in the form of the god Anubis, crouched on a naos (temple, shrine), containing jewellery and amulets. The shrine is affixed firmly to a sledge and bears the djed and tjet emblems. The carved jackal is partly gilded, the eyes are of alabaster and obsidian, the claws of silver.

55 Magnificent wooden chest with paintings in miniature, in a mannered but fascinating style. The King in his chariot conquering the Asians, his enemies from the north, a popular representation, even though the Pharaoh did not take part in the campaign. The intention was that the King should live on the Egyptians' minds as a victorious ruler. The most recent researches have shown that these scenes worked in miniature inspired the great mural compositions of the 19th dynasty.
Height of chest 17, 75 in., length 24 in.

56 Lid of a wooden chest with inlaid ivory, carved and painted. Tutankhamun is depicted with his consort. Ankhesenamun, who is offering him flowers. In the lower frieze, servant-girls are picking flowers and mandrake-fruit. Style of Amarna. Height of scene shown c. 12, 25 in. by 8 in.

57 Tutankhamun's sacerdotal throne, in the form of a folding stool with a back, covered with goldplate and inlaid with precious stones, glass-paste and ivory. In the middle of the upper frieze, the Aten-disk (solar globe, the sun) above the King's cartouches, from the Amarnan period. The seat was designed to hold a cushion. Height 40 in., width 27, 625 in., depth 17, 35 in.

58 Precious throne of wood of cedar of Lebanon, one of the most beautiful of the burial treasures. A genius symbolizes "myriad years", holding in his hands reed-shoots, symbol for "millions of years". To left and right of his head, cartouches with the royal name and the King's given name. Behind his arms, panels consisting of the King's "banner".

59 Head of unusual shape, rising from a lotus flower. Presumably the portrait of a member of the royal family, perhaps of the King. The material is painted and stuccoed wood.

60 Left: The King, wearing the red crown of Lower Egypt, is standing on a flat-bottomed boat and throwing a harpoon. Right: The King, depicted with the white crown of Upper Egypt, is standing on a panther covered with black lacquer. Both figures are gilded wooden statuettes about 29, 5 in. in height.

61 Large royal funerary bed of carved and gilded wood; not used during the King's lifetime. This bed, in the form of cheetahs, is often erroneously called the "lion-bed". Length 71, 25 in., width 36 in.

62 Head of a fabulous beast, half hippopotamus, half crocodile. Teeth and tongue of ivory, the latter stained red. This figure of the goddess Thoueris is part of the large royal funerary bed, and probably had the function of keeping away evil spirits.

63 Large royal funerary bed of carved and gilded wood. The cows symbolize the goddess Hathor. This funerary bed served purely ritual purposes and was connected with the Egyptian's dogma of rebirth. The solar disk is framed in the horns of the head.
Carter found the three funerary beds, or biers in the Antechamber, which was c. 25 ft in length, in the following order (from north to south): funerary bed in the form of cheetahs; funerary bed with figures of the sacred cow of heaven; funerary bed with figure of the goddess Thoueris. In the same room were chariots, chests, food offerings, vessels and chairs.

64 Part of the large royal funerary bed; the head is that of a cow, representing the goddess Mehurt, with the solar disk between the horns. The sacred Hathor-cow (cow of heaven) is the classical evocation of the goddess Hathor, the goddess Nut, patroness of the sky, and the goddess Mehurt, personification of the primeval waters.

65 Ushebti figures of carved and gilded cedar-wood. These statuettes were grave-gifts; their function, as the name implies, was to "answer" for the King on his last journey and in the other world, and to perform certain tasks for him in the hereafter.

66 The King's state-sandals, showing Egypt's traditional enemies, the Asians and the Negroes. "The King tramples them underfoot".

67 Ivory fan with ostrich feathers; handle in the form of a papyrus plant bearing the King's Name. The curious shape is functional and made fanning easier. Width c. 20 in., height c. 14 in.
The fan was found in an ivory and wooden box in the King's burial chamber.

68 Model boat of painted wood, with sail and steering paddles. There were several model boats found in Tutankhamun's tomb; for the most part they served religious purposes, such as "the mystic pilgrimage of the King after death". The boat shown in this picture is thought to be a model of the sailing-barge that he used for his journeys up and down the Nile.

69 The folding ivory head-rest of painted ivory, with heads of the god Bes, mishapen demon with protective powers. Height 8 in., width 7,75 in.

70 Alabaster figure in the form of a lion; effigy of the god Bes in upright position with a crown in the shape of a sealed vase. On his breast, Bes bears the King's cartouches.

71 Alabaster unguent jar with gold and ivory decorations. Two Nile-gods in upright position support trailing branches. The gods are crowned with their emblems, lotus and papyrus, and are holding two fine pillars, over which the royal uraeus-serpents are enthroned.

72 The alabaster shrine contained the canopic jars in which the four miniature coffins with the King's viscera were preserved. The shrine rests on a
gilded sled. The goddesses Isis, Nephthys, Selqet and Neith stand at the
corners of the shrine. Height of the shrine 33,5 in.

73 Two of the four unique alabaster heads of the King. They served as stoppers in the canopic chest containing the King's viscera, which were en-
trusted to the protection of four genii (sons of Horus, the falcon-headed
god of heaven), who in their turn were guarded by the four goddesses
Isis, Nephthys, Selqet and Neith. Height 9,5 in.

74 Alabaster model boat with inlay of coloured pigments. The cabin in the
form of a naos is guarded by a dwarf with a quaint wig. The canopy is
borne on pillars terminating in lotus and papyrus flowers. The prow of
the boat is in the form of a Syrian ibex with real horns, the figure of a
nude woman squats in the bows. The alabaster is inlaid with precious
stones and gold-leaf. A masterpiece.
Height of boat 14,5 in., length 11 in.

75 Triple-lamp of great charm, carved out of a single block of translucent
alabaster and depicting one open lotus-flower and two buds.
Height c. 11 in., width just under 11 in.

76 Base of an alabaster vase in the form of an ibex with real horn of a young
animal. Eyes of bronze and inlaid glass-paste, tongue of ivory stained
red; Tutenkhamon's cartouche is painted on it.

77 Elegant alabaster vase with inlay of glass-paste and semi-precious
stones, representing a band of blue lotus petals. Height about 24 in.

78 Cylindrical alabaster perfume or unguent jar; scenes of lions, bulls, dogs,
antelopes and gazelles fighting. The lid rests on two pillars representing
the god Bes. Above, resting lion with tongue of red-staines ivory hanging
out. The base rests on four heads of Negro and Asian prisoners. Height
about 10,75 in., diameter 5 in.

79 Earrings: Miniature Usekh jewellery is attached to gold studs; in the middle, bird's head of blue glass. The lower part is composed of five chains in the form of uraeus-serpents. Gold, quartz, alabaster and polychrome glaze are the materials of which they are made.
Length 4 in., width 2,5 in.

80 To the gold studs of these earrings are attached circlets of round beads made of gold and resin.

81 Rectangular pendant, with a scarab (Ateuchus sacer) between two sacred baboons. The ornament is made of gold, lapis-lazuli. turquoise and carnelian.

82 Tutankhamun between the god Ptah, as the god of pictorial artists himself a "fashioner", and the lion-goddess Sekhmet on a pectoral of gold, semiprecious stones and coloured glasspaste. On the right, the uraeus-serpent, on the left, the Horus-hawk, both with the horned sun-disk.

83 Gold bracelet inlaid with semi-precious stones. In the middle, three large scarabs of lapis-lazuli flanked by uraeus-serpents.

84 Gold bracelet inlaid with semi-precious stones. At each end, the King's cartouches; in the middle, three large scarabs, two of lapis-lazuli, one of greenish stone, flanked by four uraeus-serpents.

85 Gold pendant of lapis-lazuli and inlaid glass, showing one of the King's cartouches (Nebkheprure). Magnificent chain connecting the pendant with the counterpoise, which consists of two gold lotus-flowers.

86 The eye of the light-god Horus was called uzat, "the hale", and was a symbol of the light-god's power. It was a favourite amulet, which also protected the wearer against the "evil eye". The "magical eye" was also placed in the doorrecesses of tombs.

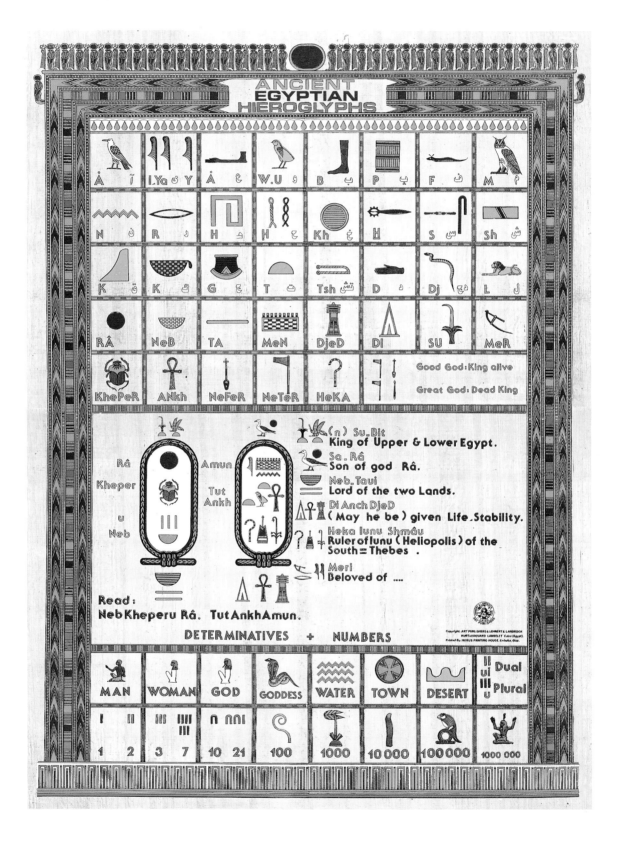

ANCIENT EGYPTIAN HIEROGLYPHS

Ả	I.Ya, Y	Ả	W.U	B	P	F	M
N	R	H	H	Kh	H	S	Sh
K	K	G	T	Tsh	D	Dj	L
RÂ	NeB	TA	MeN	DjeD	DI	SU	MeR
KhePeR	ANkh	NeFeR	NeTeR	HeKA		Good God: King alive / Great God: Dead King

Râ
Kheper
u
Neb

Amun
Tut
Ankh

(n) Su.Bit
King of Upper & Lower Egypt.

Sa. Râ
Son of god Râ.

Neb. Taui
Lord of the two Lands.

Di Anch DjeD
(May he be) given Life.Stability.

Heka Iunu Shmâu
Ruler of Iunu (Heliopolis) of the South = Thebes .

Meri
Beloved of ....

Read:
Neb Kheperu Râ. Tut Ankh Amun.

DETERMINATIVES + NUMBERS

MAN	WOMAN	GOD	GODDESS	WATER	TOWN	DESERT	Dual / Plural
1	2	3 7	10 21	100	1000	10 000	100 000	1000 000